There IS a better way of living!

There IS a better way of living!

A sensible approach to personal and family growth

Sidney Gerhardt
& Elizabeth G. McKay

A Continuum Book
THE SEABURY PRESS • NEW YORK

The Seabury Press, Inc.
815 Second Avenue
New York, N.Y. 10017

Printed in the United States of America

Library of Congress Cataloging in Publication Data

Gerhardt, Sidney, 1927-
    There is a better way of living! a sensible approach to personal and family
    growth

    (A Continuum book)
    1. Family. 2. Interpersonal relations. 3. Socialization. I. McKay,
Elizabeth G., 1940-   joint author. II. Title.
HQ734.G39   301.42'7   75-14443
ISBN 0-8164-9268-9

to Fran and Bob

Contents

Preface

Are you satisfied with yourself, fulfilled with the useful life you're leading, certain there is nothing missing in your feelings about yourself or about your relationships with family and friends? Will your children have the opportunity to face the future with the essentials of life to carry them through life's unavoidable hurts because you have taught them well? If so, put down this book. It's not for you.

If, on the other hand, you feel there may be something missing, some unidentifiable ingredient lacking in you, some kind of itching dissatisfaction that you can't quite locate, then read on. There *is* a better way to live.

We are both members of Psychiatric and Counseling Associates in Stamford, Connecticut. This book is the result of observations made over the years by us and our associates. We have used "I" when presenting our opinions. "We" is used in presenting material common to you, the reader, and the authors.

Bombarded on all sides with crises, controversies, and changes, people come through our doors overburdened with personal problems. They know that something is wrong with their lives, that something is missing, but they do not know what it is. I have observed over the years a common absence. All these people are missing the richness of interpersonal relationships.

9

We all have areas of weakness—their effect is a matter of degree. Despite the rash of books and articles on how to improve our lives, few, if any, present an understandable description of the weaknesses which prevent us from doing this. If our deficiency is great, it is likely to prevent us from attempting to find a better way of living. We need to learn what our weaknesses are, why we have them, and what resources are available for counterbalancing them, so that we can reduce the impact that they have on us and those around us, especially our children. To soften their potency, we have to strive to understand the present meaning of our unpleasant memories and relationships.

We were all students long ago in the primary classroom of our families. Our parents were our teachers of emotional response. By imitating them, or their surrogates, we learned how to behave. We cannot blame them for our lacks, for how did they learn? Did they know all they were supposed to know? Of course not. They learned primarily from their parents who had weaknesses themselves. We were not deliberately taught to be ineffective; rather, weaknesses have been transmitted through ignorance.

In a society which idolizes individuality, the self-made person, and solitary resolution of one's own problems, it is unrealistically assumed that we know all we need to know about being a person by the time we are ready for marriage and parenthood.

What I hope to show is that we often do not know what we are supposed to know, that we transmit our weaknesses to our children, that we can recognize these weaknesses, and that there are ways of lessening them to improve the quality of our lives.

This book is written for those who wish to be students of themselves, who wish to learn new ways of striving for inner growth, who want to try to learn what they are supposed to know for themselves and for the children they may have.

Are you ready? *You* will have to make the effort to recognize yourself in some of the situations I describe, and it is *you* who must put the lessons into practice.

S. G.
E. McK.

Acknowledgments

We are especially grateful to Helen Marie Grady for her creative and thoughtful suggestions, which have contributed so much to this book. For their cheerful questioning, understanding, and patience, we thank Alicia, Mindy, and Teena Gerhardt, and John, Mary Pat, and Elizabeth McKay.

I / I Can't Get Started

Special days mark the cycle of each passing year. Children ponder: "Will my birthday ever come?" "When will I be grown up?" They are puzzled when adults comment: "Is it September already? Where has the time gone?" They would wonder even more if they could hear our inner voices: "I'm grown up now. When will life begin to have meaning?"

"It's a struggle," Nick, age thirty-three, says. "It's always been a struggle. Even now, I don't know how to get started!"

Nick may sound extreme, but how many of us are very much like him? How many of us just can't get started? We can't seem to begin—a conversation with a stranger, making a new friend or writing to an old one, getting back into the job after a vacation, studying for an exam, taking up tennis or fixing a fence, changing a job—the countless things that put meaning into life.

We all admire those who take risks, who meet life head-on with humor and warmth, who don't let their problems get them down, who somehow possess an inner peace and cheerfully share it, laughing at their frailties and delighting in their accomplishments—people who always seem to know what to do, how to do it, and go about doing it. *They* know how to get started. What's

15

their secret? We feel that we're supposed to be like them
but we don't know how.

In all areas of life, we assume everyone has certain
basic knowledge. Whan a woman gives birth to a child,
we assume she knows how to be a mother. When someone is missing knowledge that we assume everyone
should know, we are surprised, bewildered, and sometimes shocked. I experienced this myself.

While in a supermarket, recently, I noticed an elderly
woman looking at a shelf and glancing around as if for
help. As I walked by, she asked, "Will you help me? I
need some peanut butter." For a split second I thought
that she must be blind. Just a few feet ahead of her was
enough peanut butter—crunchy, smooth, big jars, little
jars, this brand, that one—to keep a playground of children in sandwiches for a month.

"Of course," I said. "They're right up there."

She walked up to the shelf and picked up the nearest
jar. "Thanks, I thought it was around here, but I just
wasn't sure because I don't know how to read."

As I watched her go off towards the cashier with
that special walk of plump, little old ladies who have
just accomplished something important to them, my
mouth fell open. The lady simply could not read. She
did not know what I had assumed everyone knows.

Obviously, most people who do not know what everyone is supposed to know are aware of their weaknesses.
They have discovered how difficult daily life can be
without basic knowledge, and they either attempt to
learn what they did not learn as children, or they com-
pensate in other ways.

As another example, when we were in school, teachers constantly told us where our strengths, weaknesses
and potentials were. If we had trouble learning our numbers, if we couldn't do arithmetic in second grade, our

teachers not only encouraged us but probably gave us extra work to do at home. If that didn't work, they might have given us an F (today it's an NS for "Needs Strengthening") and perhaps found an older child to tutor us. All kinds of arguments would be used to persuade us to improve our arithmetic. "When you become an adult, if you can't do basic arithmetic, how will you pay your bills; how will you know if you're being paid a fair wage; how will you buy a shirt without fear of being cheated; how will you pay the rent, or even keep score during a ball game?" While such arguments had little meaning to us at age eight, they surely matter to us now. We may never have gone on to learn calculus, but most of us have been motivated to learn the fundamental concepts of numbers and can at least take care of our own money. Most of us know what we are supposed to know in this area.

Just as we would find life difficult without any grasp of arithmetic, and just as the elderly woman who could not read had trouble with a simple task, so do we often suffer emotionally because of insufficient emotional knowledge. The difference is that we know if we can't add, just as the old woman knew she couldn't read and could easily ask for help. But if our emotional education is deficient, too often we are not aware of what is missing. Not only do we not know what we are supposed to know, we may not even be aware that we are ignorant in that area.

We tend to hide emotional incompleteness even from ourselves. We don't want to expose that kind of weakness to anyone. Out of a mistaken notion of self-preservation, we nail up a sign that says: *No Trespassing. Violators Will Be Turned Away!* Behind the sign, deep within ourselves, we waste our energies in an endless battle to make up what is missing, to satisfy ourselves, to give meaning to our lives.

Even as there were many ways for us to learn arithmetic, there are also many ways to master our emotional insufficiency. Unfortunately, we tend to find ways merely to cover our emptiness rather than to fill it. In so doing, we are doomed to failure because the emptiness continues to demand fulfillment. What keeps us from getting started is simply that *we do not know what that emptiness is;* we only know that we are hurting.

From the moment of birth, we try to keep pain of every kind from controlling us. If we cannot defend ourselves from pain, we will not survive. In childhood we set our own unique patterns of response to the outside world, and establish individual ways of mastering the pleasures and pains of daily life. Think of the pattern as a patchwork quilt—not the usual kind, but one highlighted with the down of velvet, the luster of silk, the sturdiness of canvas, the grace of chiffon, the warmth of wool, and the practicality of cotton—all in shades and tones that run the gamut from sunshine to India ink. Imagine that quilt with a piece left out. With age, the gap will grow greater; the fabric around it will fray; the whole quilt will be in danger of falling apart. Our emotional pattern is something like this. Just as we can fold the quilt so that no one can see the hole, we will have to curl our knees up to our chins, so we can hide the gap in our emotional pattern. Not knowing what we're supposed to know keeps us from getting started with real repair of our private quilts.

Nick, who doesn't know how to get started, is, like so many of us, a man who harbors ambition but becomes discouraged, who gets along well with people yet avoids making close contact, who loves his family but has difficulty expressing his feelings. Uncertain of any decision he has to make, Nick is compliant to the point of being submissive; striving to avoid disapproval, he rarely, if ever, expresses anger. At best, he is a man without zest. He is a man who cries inside.

While Nick is aware that wishing will not make even his simplest dreams come true, that he can fulfill them only by active mastering, at thirty-three he's exhausted by the effort. His goals seem no nearer. In fact, he feels that despite all his effort he hasn't really begun.

Where has all this man's vitality gone? At his age, he should be at the peak of his powers. He is well-spoken, attractive, and sensitive. Why does he avoid closeness with others? He works long and hard, yet has no sense of achievement or fulfillment. Why?

An oldest son, Nick was born in a small town in Pennsylvania into a family both religiously and culturally committed to its Greek origins. His mother and father had met in Philadelphia, but chose to live close to her mother's large and sprawling family in the country.

Nick remembers his early childhood as a time of happiness. While his father had to stay in the city during much of the week, coming home only on weekends, Nick really didn't miss him with so many uncles, aunts, and cousins around. He recalls the times spent with his grandmother with warmth. "She made me feel special," he remembers affectionately. I had the feeling that he should have been speaking of his mother.

About his mother, he said, "Well, I remember she was always busy. I guess we three kids were a lot of work. I guess you could say she was strong-willed and unbending. I can remember her telling me when I was ready for kindergarten, how hard I would have to work in school, so that I could go to work in a suit when I became a man. She was very strict about everything." Nick's schoolwork and his bettering of himself were all that mattered to Nick's mother. She looked upon fun as a costly lux-

ury that took time away from study. Friends were dis-
tractions, and unwelcome, but somehow Nick managed
to do well in school and to have friends, too.

When Nick was nine, the family moved about 200
miles to another city where his father had an opportunity
to run his own restaurant. Grandmother, uncles, aunts,
and cousins had brought some warmth into the chilly
family atmosphere, but moving ended that. While Nick's
father was a warm person, he too had an unbending attitude toward work. The raising of the children was left
to his wife. Restriction, prohibition, and hard work were
Nick's daily diet.

As he put it, "Building up the business robbed me of
an adolescence." After school, he would have to help
downstairs in the restaurant. The only excuse accepted
for not setting the tables or washing the dishes was
schoolwork. Even when he wanted to join the swimming
team, his mother found it unacceptable and a total
waste of time. Nor did she accept his new friends. Nick
would wait until his parents were asleep and then sneak
out to be with his friends. Even when Nick started at the
city college, his mother did not let up. His friends were
still not welcome and he was still expected to help in the
restaurant. Finally, he was allowed to see his friends
without sneaking out, but when he did go, his mother
never failed to warn him of trouble or to criticize his
friends. As he put it, "I still had the same feeling, that I
was sneaking out."

In his sophomore year, Melissa entered Nick's life.
Long rambling walks through the city, hours spent in
deep conversation kept the relationship growing. Together they would build the kind of home and family
that each had always wanted. As a belated Christmas
present to themselves, they eloped on the twenty-eighth
of December, 1961. He was twenty. She was seventeen.

Nick's mother felt that her hope was shattered. He hadn't finished college. How could he be what *she* wanted?

Refusing his father's offer to work in the restaurant, Nick got a job with a suit and tie, as his mother wanted. He started as a clerk in a bank and gradually worked up to teller.

When he came to see me, Nick and Melissa were still living in the apartment they had found when their third child was due. He was still a bank teller although he had recently completed college. He knew he should get a better paying job because they could never afford the house they both wanted on the salary he was making.

When I asked Nick how he thought I could help him, he said, "I just can't seem to decide what I want to do. What I really want is someone to tell me what I should do to make my family happy and be happy myself. But, I just don't know how to get started at changing things. There's something missing, but I don't know what it is."

Where is the gap in Nick's pattern that makes him so unable to begin? His deficiency causes him to do nothing to improve his life. This, in turn, causes his wife to keep trying to make him decide. Underneath it all he really wants her to keep pressuring him, as his mother had done in his early life. He has an insatiable need for someone to set his sights and pull the trigger so that he can move towards realizing his goals. This inability to do this for himself is the hole in his quilt, the piece left out in the making of his pattern in childhood.

As a small boy, Nick obeyed his mother out of fear of disapproval, fear of losing her affection. She told him what to do, when to do it, and how to do it. Nick gradually, but thoroughly, took over her restrictive opinions and demands. In his desire to please her, these demands became so much a part of his own fabric that they now prevented him from having the free rein he needed to fulfill his own aspirations. His mother's opinions and demands are the patches of the quilt that we can see. Her influence was so strong that Nick's impressions from his absent and submissive father had been overwhelmed.

Nick is right when he says that he was "robbed of his adolescence." Adolescence is the time when we learn to think for ourselves, to start to fulfill our own acceptable strivings. Certainly Nick's desire to be a swimmer is a perfectly ordinary one for a growing boy. But his mother's view of swimming as a waste of time gave Nick the impression that this particular aspiration itself was unsuitable.

While others might have rebelled, Nick stuck with the only solution he knew that would keep him in his parents' favor. He swallowed the striving along with his hurt and anger at being disappointed. Eventually, this negative method of mastering became automatic for him. His current sluggish attitude stems from the emphasis on fearful obedience, caution, and inhibition of his own desires throughout his growing years.

Perhaps most illustrative of Nick's dilemma is his occupation. When I talked with Nick about his job, he freely admitted that, at Melissa's urging and with her constant support, he managed to endure the hardship of night school to achieve his degree in business so that he would be able to improve his job. Two years later he's still a bank teller.

Even though his dream is to live on a small farm, raise some kind of cash crop, and work part-time as a recreational supervisor, Nick has plunged himself into a jacket-and-tie, nine-to-five, city occupation against his own inner desires. In fulfilling his mother's ambitions, his own ambitions are still unacceptable. As a result, he functions at a half-measures level. He feels neither the pleasure of success at his work nor the pleasure of having put effort into attaining success. The lack of satisfaction makes him angry at himself, but he can't express this anger. His aggressive feelings are folded inside. His inability to be openly angry makes him even more angry. The vicious circle of anger and counteranger drains him.

Nick's emotional pattern contains many strengths that he is not using to their full extent. He possesses a resiliency that will enable him to recover vitality and determination when tension and fear are reduced. At times, he is able to share himself, to "give away" of himself to his wife and children; he needs to learn to extend this sharing within his family and into other parts of his life.

Nick is searching for someone to tell him what to do so that he and his family can be "happy." Others can give him advice, but no one can ever give him self-direction. No one can activate him, he must do that himself. First he needs to gain an understanding of his own weaknesses and strengths, then identify his acceptable strivings. In examining them, he has to assess their attainability.

Is his goal of "happiness" attainable? So many of us spend our lives in the pursuit of the impossible. We would all love to be happy, but happiness for some implies perfection. If we chase perfection, we run endlessly after a mirage. Life as pursuit will only bring us great pain; wanting more makes us need more. We will just never get there. Inner satisfaction, a sense of worth, a useful life, these are achievable. Total happiness is not.

Perhaps we should look at happiness another way. In a single day we can be happy or unhappy many times. If we see a close friend we haven't seen for some time, we are delighted. If, later on in the day, we hear that someone else we care for has had an accident, we are unhappy. Happinesss or pleasure happens to us on occasion, in certain situations. Unhappiness or pain happens in the same way. Our goal is to achieve a balance in our lives where happiness outweighs sadness and pain. For Nick to achieve that balance, he has a great deal of thinking to do about himself. He may have to acquire a new dimension.

Is it possible for Nick to add on what he does not know? He had never left the primary classroom of his family. He had taken in his mother's impressions, assumed her strivings as his own, but never separated from them by adding on his own desires. Because he had not made this separation, he had never been able to fully utilize society, the secondary classroom, to teach him what his childhood had not taught him. He never completed the process of growing up emotionally because he was never able to express his acceptable strivings. He is now unable to activate himself and thus has no means of winning that sense of self-worth that is the source of meaning in life. He is not taking in or giving away enough emotional nourishment to give his life the balance that will carry him through the inevitable times of pain and sorrow.

Are you, like Nick, always caught between the same set of pros and cons, unhappy with yourself and your life, knowing only that there must be a better way to live than your way? If you see yourself in Nick, then you, too, need first to understand the major insufficiency in your emotional pattern that is keeping you from going beyond the primary classroom to add on what you are missing.

"Mastering" is the process by which we take in and respond to the outside world. It marks the form and fabric of our quilts. If you were not allowed to express your acceptable strivings, you were not taught to master constructively, and your primary emotional education may not be completed. If you are unable to take in enough nourishment to activate yourself so that you bring balance into your life, you first need to examine how and what you *did* learn. You just don't know how to get started because you have learned to avoid rather than to participate in life.

The past has too much meaning for Nick in the present. The intensity of Nick's disappointment in the past has remained with him because he learned too well how to avoid expressing himself. He rigidly continues to master in the same way in order to avoid future disappointment. Without flexibility, unable to express himself, he is unable to establish the kind of relationships that might teach him what he did not have the opportunity to learn in the primary classroom. He will have to soften the meaning of his past if he wants to be open enough to become involved in the richness of personal relationships.

Our relationships with our parents are the foundations of our emotional patterns. I will explain the process of how we learn from them, but it is up to you to discover what was missing in your particular emotional education that prevents you from striving to put meaning into your life. You will have to identify what it is that you don't know. You will have to strive to understand the meaning of your past.

Let us begin.

2 / You Can't Change the Past

How has it happened that some of us have such thread-bare, thin, raggedy quilts that give no warmth and bring no comfort? When someone wants to see it, we show only the smallest bit—the strongest and sturdiest, per-haps, so that we can hide the shabbiness of the rest. How is it that we do not know what we are supposed to know to make our quilts whole? We do not know be-cause we have never learned.

To make them whole, we need to learn the process of mastering. As I said in the previous chapter, mastering is the way we take in and respond to the world outside us. It is a learned behavior which may be positive or negative. If we have learned positive ways to respond to the world—and there are many—our patterns will be rich. If, however, we know only a few ways, or if our master-ing is more negative than positive, our quilts will be drab and incomplete.

The external world affects us in countless ways. In the physical sphere the effects of the world are obvious. In the area of the intellect, we know what we know be-cause we assimilate it from what is going on around us. We take in what is taught us. It becomes so much a part of us that we cannot imagine ourselves without our knowledge. We externalize what we know by using it. We continually add to it, building on to what we already know. We were taught to read very early in life. We have assimilated that knowledge and made it our own. We use it in all areas of our lives. We cannot conceive of ourselves as illiterate.

In our emotional life a similar process is at work. When we are introduced to someone new, we take in how he looks, his voice, his whole attitude. He activates a response within us which we then externalize in some way. If he is warm and friendly, we respond with warmth, which we show with a smile, giving back our own warmth and friendliness. If previous experience has made him cold and ungiving, we are liable to be polite but aloof in return. Thus, what we take in from the outside world activates an internal response which we then externalize in some way.

If this first attempt to restore our balance with the outside world does not satisfy us, we try alternatives. For instance, if one warm, tentative response to someone receives a cold, ungiving, inappropriate reply, we may draw away in dissatisfaction, ending contact immediately. On the other hand, we may try the alternative of further extending ourselves by showing more warmth and interest in an attempt to win a more appropriate and satisfying answer. This process of taking in, responding internally, externalizing that response, changing it, if necessary, to satisfy our needs—this is mastering.

The most basic mastering is for self-preservation. A few days old, still wrinkled and red, even in the stillness of sleep, the newborn's fingers flutter. He wakes, wiggles, struggles with his blanket. No answer from the outer world is affecting him; he is not being fed. His internal

response is one of intense discomfort. He is hungry. His
body grows rigid, he wails with all his power—what a
surprisingly large, angry sound comes from such small-
ness! You can see the tension in his whole body. He is
externalizing his internal discomfort, trying to restore
his equilibrium, trying to ease his pain. He cannot feed
himself; his means of self-mastering are far too limited.
But, if he must wait, what can he do? A tiny flailing hand
finds his mouth. He grows still; inner balance is tem-
porarily restored as he sucks on his own hand. No fulfillment has come from the outside, but *he has done
something himself* to attempt to ease his pain.

This last point is crucial in our learning to master.
Like the infant, we have to actively do something ourselves. In this lies the feeling of self-worth, the inner
satisfaction that will uplift our self-esteem. We can give
ourselves our own emotional nourishment.

For example, take the man who wants to be more understanding of his wife. He knows that he habitually
puts her down for not doing things the way he wants
them. To learn a new way of mastering, he must not only
be aware of his weakness and desire to change, but he
needs to work against his own irritation. When his wife
does something that angers him—for instance, when
dinner isn't ready for him when he gets home—he nor-
mally responds with a deprecation: "Damn it! The least
you could do is have dinner ready when I want it." If
he truly wants to change, the instant he takes in what
has happened and feels that familiar anger start to rise
he must counterbalance this with the idea: "I'm not
going to let this happen to me." This confrontation with
what is coming in will soften his internal, angry response.
In meeting his anger, he does not necessarily eliminate
it; rather, he controls it. As a result his external response
is also softened. He might say, "I'm hungry. Are we

going to eat soon?" His wife knows how he feels; she gets the message, but in changing the way he has given it to her, he has not precipitated a conflict. She does not feel she has to fight back, so her reaction will also be different. Chances are they will both eat sooner without a battle to give them both indigestion.

By actively working against his own weakness, the husband will feel an inner satisfaction at having accomplished his aim to be more understanding. In uplifting his own self-esteem, he is supplying his own emotional nourishment. The rewards for his effort will give him the energy to continue trying. Moreover, he receives further rewards from his wife, who is free to respond positively because the message is altered so that it no longer arouses anger in her. What we see here is the beginning of a change for the better in the whole relationship.

Throughout our daily lives, we must put our own effort into making a better life. As babies we could not do it, but we tried even then. Infancy and childhood are the times for learning to master well. Our weaknesses come from not learning enough. Often the opportunity simply is not there. An infant cannot fill even his most basic need—food. At this early stage he wants what he wants *when* he wants it. He expects instant gratification.

It is here, in this earliest period of our lives, that the power of the mother shows itself in full force. Because she is usually the one who fulfills our first, most basic need, our bond with her is primary. Because she is this source, we gradually realize that her approval of us is essential. She has the power to feed us, and the power to take our food away. To win her approval, we eventually put aside that demand for instant pleasure. As

we become aware of her importance, we learn to tolerate waiting for pleasure in order to gain the warmth
and comfort of her attention. As in the case of Nick, we
internalize our mother's prohibitions or her warmth or
both.

Our newborn is older now. The world is a fascinating
place. He spends a long time examining his hands and
feet. He has discovered that he can make the most fascinating noises with his tongue and mouth. Of primary
importance to him is the now familiar face of his mother
smiling down at him. He values, too, the hands that keep
him clean, the warmth and safety he feels when his
mother holds him. If her voice is harsh, it frightens him,
but when she smiles or sings, he reaches for her, smiling,
pulling at her clothing, her hair, any part of her within
his grasp. When he is upset, sometimes just her presence is enough to comfort him.

As he develops from infancy, the child gains more resources for mastering. His mother is his first teacher.
She makes an indelible impression on him. If she never
makes the child wait for what he wants, he will always
seek instant pleasure, never learning that he must respond with his own effort to gain real satisfaction. If she
rarely gives him what he needs, if he cannot maintain
that feeling of warmth, he will forever search for it without really being sure what it is. In time, the child can
crawl to or away from something; he can accept, or refuse. His mother's reactions tell him whether his actions
are acceptable or unacceptable. If she is pleased, he
can do it, but if it angers her, he must not.

As the child grows, a second figure usually enters his
life. The child becomes increasingly aware of another
controlling and constant presence in his environment.
For the child, his father is a model of what a man is.
How much the child learns from his father depends on

how interested his father is in him. The child will learn
what to do, what not to do, as well as how to do it in an
effort to win approval as his awareness of his father increases. A boy discovers that he is male like his father.
His father shows him how to become a man and how to
relate to a woman. A girl has her mother as a model of
a woman, but she learns what a man is and how to respond to him from her father.

How then did we learn to control what we take in from
the outside world and to respond to it? We learned from
the impressions of others that we took in. They charted
the development of our personalities. As the most central,
strongest external forces in our childhood world, our
parents made the most forcible impressions on us. Their
impact on us is tremendously potent. We internalized
their personalities; it was their desires, both overtly and
covertly expressed, that became part of us. We learned
by *imitating* to please them. These *imitation impressions* were considered acceptable in the past and worthy
of continued imitation in the future. These impressions
taught us how to control what we took in and how to respond to it. Keeping in mind that the mother's impressions are still primary, that the personality undergoes
changes during growth, and that the father's impressions increase in importance with age, it should be noted
that one or the other parent might make a stronger impression, or be more determined to influence us. When
this happens, the impressions of the more influential
parent will tend to block those of the weaker one.

New ways of mastering are learned through new experiences, all building on previous ones. With repetition and addition, the patches of our quilts are pieced in,
the quality dependent on how well and in what ways we
have learned to master.

Unfortunately, for many of us the learning process is

incomplete. The impressions from our parents did not teach us enough. We were cheated in a sense. Why? *Because they did not know* the most positive ways of mastering themselves and those are the ways we incorporated. They did not deliberately leave us in ignorance. It is the rare parent who purposefully hurts his children. The rents and ravels, the gaping insufficiencies exist in our emotional patterns because our parents could not teach us what they did not know themselves. We have not learned new responses in changed situations because we have not learned to take in what is necessary from the outside world.

How often have we said to our children, "You just don't listen to me!" Our words fall on deaf ears. There is no reaction. What we don't realize is that our child's deafness is a protection. He wants to avoid disapproval. He is afraid to let us in, because of his inner fear and tension. If we shout louder in our frustration, we are actually reinforcing his refusal to take in our words. We are proving to him with each increasing decibel that his armor is working. Beyond that he begins to realize that he is exerting a control over us. His action is causing us to rant and rave. The more we do it, the stronger proof he has that his way of mastering is working. His silence, his inaction is powerful. While he is maintaining his equilibrium, we are losing ours. Potent yes, but it is not constructive mastering. With repetition he may become overdependent on this negative kind of mastering. He will deny himself the opportunities of developing more positive methods. He may be caught in the exaggeration of a single mode of mastering that will deny him involvement, self-achievement, and the flexibility he will need to have close relationships with others. A time may come when he will be unable to let in the essentials of warmth and affection, and he will become incapable of responding with his own warmth.

This could have happened to Andy. His mother realized that things were getting out of hand as successive teachers reported how frightened Andy was, and each report card escalated the tension in the family atmosphere. More importantly, Andy's father was willing to admit that perhaps the blame for Andy's behavior could not be placed on his nine-year-old shoulders. "Maybe, I'm doing something wrong, or maybe something's missing. I just don't know."

His mother, a warm and loving person, had given Andy good impressions during his early years. But as Andy grew older, the need for his father's approval increased. To the father, Andy's performance in school was all important. He equated good grades with being a good child. Excelling in school was the only way Andy could win his father's approval. Each day Andy trudged home, the day's work in his hand. Each evening Andy's father examined it, questioning each mistake, thundering at him for his poor performance.

When Andy first started school, the angry bursts activated fear and tension within him. At first, he had tried to "give away" of himself, to make an effort, to get involved. His grades were average. It seemed that no matter how hard he tried, it wasn't enough to please his father. With each outburst the level of fear and tension accumulated. Andy had to restore the balance within himself. To do this, to de-escalate and bring his inner discomfort to a more tolerable level, Andy tried an alternative response. He stopped trying. In school he sat in class and daydreamed about a utopia where there was no school, about being someone else, about anything that passed the time. At home, he stood quietly while his father's fury crashed about him.

Previously, Andy's tentative attempts at positive mastering were met with a barrage. Since his effort wasn't good enough, Andy had to feel that he was inadequate. "What's wrong with me?" Repetition brought him to the conclusion, "I must be bad." Effort didn't pay. So by refusing to get involved, by avoiding, Andy discovered he could do away with the risk of further criticism of his inadequacy. Punishments actually reinforced his avoidance. Andy felt guilty: "I must be bad." Punishment took away his guilt. Moreover, it was better than no relationship with his father. Since he could not win his father's approval, at least his father would help him control the badness in him.

Andy's mother tried to ease the pressure on the boy without undermining his father. She found herself in a "Kissinger role," shuttling back and forth, negotiating for family friendliness. As the situation worsened, Andy's fourth-grade teacher and the school psychologist suggested that the parents seek help. They came to me.

Andy's father was willing to examine himself, to find the weaknesses in his emotional pattern, to discover what he did not know that he was supposed to know. He soon became aware that it was his own lack of performance, his own unfilled aspiration that made him so critical of his son. He had to recognize and learn to do something about his own acceptable strivings, rather than putting them on Andy's back. As Andy's father gradually added on what he did not know, Andy, too, learned new ways of mastering. A parent is that powerful.

With the change in expectations, Andy's father replaced anger with encouragement. Andy could safely let encouragement in. The internal response to encouragement is confidence. As confidence gradually replaced the feeling of inadequacy and badness, Andy responded by putting some effort into his school work. He escalated, that is, he took an upward and outward action to receive worthiness and praise. As his effort was rewarded with praise, he was able to "give away" more and more, to really get involved.

Andy's father began bringing me his son's report cards, not as a judgment on Andy, but rather to show me his own improvement. Andy's grades had become his father's! How well his father learned new ways of mastering was reflected on Andy's report card.

Children learn to master by imitation. Besides their parents, most take on many different models in the ordinary course of childhood—a special teacher, an aunt or uncle, a family friend—people whose particular characteristics appeal to them. Often the additional model has traits that a parent does not have. A child with an energetic, ebullient father may especially admire a soft-spoken uncle. Often the admired person has qualities the child feels he does not possess. Thus, a child who tends to be serious may be drawn to a family friend who has a raucous sense of humor. By imitating others outside the family, the child adds on to the impressions given him by his parents. This childhood process of picking up favorable characteristics, the admiration that leads to imitation, is one that we can carry on throughout our lives. It is one way of enriching ourselves.

Despite these alternative models, parental acceptance and approval remain extremely important to the child as the source of his sense of self-worth. So important, in fact, that he sometimes misreads the message. Yet parents are often unaware of the impact they have on their children. For example, bantering, that kind of humor touched with sarcasm which is more characteristically a masculine type of behavior, cannot be understood by a child. Intended as a sign of affection, it is invariably misread by the child.

If Andy had come home with the news that he was second in his class and his father lightly responded,

"That's fine, but why aren't you first?" Andy would have misunderstood him. The second part of the statement negates the first. Andy's view would be that what he had done was still not good enough to please his father, thus wiping out the satisfaction and boost to his self-esteem that his accomplishment had originally given him.

What happens if the child does not win his parents' acceptance; if he feels he cannot please them? If no alternative attempt wins their approval, he may stop the assimilation process, refusing to abide by previous impressions. In an effort to lessen his inner discomfort, he will stop imitating his parents. He will behave in the opposite way. The child may assume substitute models and learn from them (as Nick did with his grandmother). But if his parents repair their quilts by acquiring new ways of mastering, and alter their responses, the child will turn back to them, assuming them as models once again. Their approval is still his primary goal. If they make it possible by consistently striving to understand the child's needs, he will imitate them in preference to others. In this way, parental care and understanding usually create opportunities for a child to learn openness to the world around him and empathy with others. The story of Shirley exemplifies how imitation may pause, what may happen, how the process may resume, and the result on the child.

It wasn't that Shirley's mother didn't care for her; it was simply that Shirley couldn't see how. Her mother was cold, strong-willed, domineering, more interested in outside activities than in her home. Shirley did her utmost to please her. Never naughty, Shirley was a docile child who would not dream of going off on her own. Luckily for Shirley there was an elderly woman who lived next door and who was blessed with gentle humor and lively imagination. She showered the little girl with warmth and interest. When her mother scolded her, Shirley's fears and tears were wiped away as she sat on her neighbor's ample lap.

When Shirley was in kindergarten, her sister was born. Despite the usual sibling rivalry, Shirley was glad that her mother was spending more time at home. Besides that, the baby was interesting. Shirley continued in her passive ways.

At two, Shirley's sister began to do the most daring things. One day, she threw all her toys out the window. Another time, she splashed so much water in the bathtub that even the ceiling dripped! Then she decorated half the kitchen with a surrealistic mural of orange on white. Naturally her mother scolded, but Shirley began to notice that the scolding *she* received for spots on her dress seemed a little worse.

Shirley's impressions from her mother were clear to her. She must be careful and obey. However, in response to her efforts to please, Shirley had been taking in a feeling of coldness, of not being wanted. The imitation process paused. Shirley became more and more cranky. The formerly quiet and cooperative child threw one temper tantrum, then another. "You're the meanest mother in the whole wide world. I'm not going to do what you say." Off she would flounce to her room. Punishment did nothing to improve her disposition.

Crushed by the discovery that her husband was having an affair, disorganized, panicky, Shirley's mother came to see me. Her fear of losing her husband made her eager to understand what was missing in her family life. She came to realize that her negative impressions were all over the family; no one else could assert himself, while she was too involved with her own concerns. Admitting her faults, learning to share herself, to give

away the essentials of warmth and interest created a new
atmosphere within the family. Patiently, she started to
include Shirley in some of her activities. She gave up
other activities. The family began to do things together
—a trip to the park, to the children's zoo, to a Disney
movie on a rainy Sunday afternoon. Gone were Shirley's
temper tantrums, whining, and complaints. Cooperation
returned. The imitation process resumed, but something new was added—Shirley started to do things on her
own, to voice her own opinions, to ask questions, and to
talk about how she felt.

Shirley's mother showed me her Mother's Day card.
Shirley had picked it out herself. It was the kind that
catalogues a mother's virtues, but Shirley hadn't left it
at that. She had circled *Always There* and wrote in
"Often"; *Scolds Me When I'm Wrong* received "Not So
Much"; *Listens to My Troubles* merited "Much More";
and *Loves Me* won a resounding "*YES!*"

When docility had not won her mother's approval,
Shirley's imitating eventually paused. Her response
wasn't working to win the warmth and affection she
wanted. Instead inner frustration was accumulating.
Shirley tried an alternative. She stopped trying to please
and externalized her anger and frustration. This at least
gave her some comfort. With the change in her mother,
Shirley responded with a return to an effort to please
her. When her mother responded with affection, Shirley
was able to escalate, to take that effort a step further.
In response to the feeling of being wanted, Shirley was
able to "give away" of herself. She dared to take the
risk of doing things for herself, to talk about how she
felt, to give warmth and affection in return. She had begun to learn new and positive mastering by imitating
her mother.

Society unrealistically assumes that since we know how to feed and clothe a child, we also know how to teach him to be a person. We cannot blame our parents for what they did not teach us. It was not a deliberate omission; they did not know. If they did not know they could not teach us.

As imperfect as our parents may have been, their impressions are part of us. Emotionally, we are all male and female, mother and father, perhaps more of one than the other. Our parents are truly our primary, most powerful teachers. Our later learning can add on, can modify, but it can never remove the indelible marks they have left on us. But the meaning of these marks can change as we grow. For example, in later childhood, through school and outside contacts in the secondary classroom, the child may imitate admired characteristics in other models in a kind of experimentation, but parental acceptance and restraints are still of extreme importance. It is in adolescence that we first face ourselves. With one foot in the dependent, secure childhood world and the other reaching for maturity, we spend years taking the emotional step out of the primary classroom, of the home. Some people never quite complete the separation. It is this that prevents them from being able to activate themselves. Physical adolescence occurs in a specific time frame; emotional adolescence does not. Pushing children out of their homes will not give them emotional maturity; they must take this step themselves—a difficult, usually painful process.

At the center of the separation process lies the person's view of himself. Looking in the mirror may tell a child that he has a nose like his father, which would be okay if it weren't for his eyes. They may be like his mother's—too close together. Looking inside himself, he can see their impressions—many he may not like. If he rejects them, cannot forgive them, even hates them, he is at war with himself. These are the emotional storms of adolescence. He cuts the emotional umbilical cord by accepting himself as he is. This acceptance leads to a striving to make meaning out of life's situations. Aware of what his limitations are, the child can actively do something about modifying those aspects of himself that he would like to improve, and can add on through imitation in the secondary classroom what he has failed to learn in the primary one.

Thus, a son, accepting the fact that his father was a parent in name only, may not know how to be a good father. If he has made the separation from the primary classroom, knowing from experience what *not* to do, he can be a good father himself. His father may have been cruel or cold, but despite those impressions, he does not have to be that way himself. In adding on what he failed to learn, the young man may start by doing the opposite: he may imitate another; he may read; and he may discuss and compare his ideas with his friends. In other words, he utilizes the resources of the secondary classroom to make up for what he did not learn in the primary.

Are you able to do this? Have you completed the separation process? If you really want to gain that inner impetus that will enable you to activate yourself, it is not too late.

3/ It's Going to Happen to You

The very young person thinks: "Grown-ups really have it made. They can do everything they want to do." The adolescent softens this a bit with the thought that life will be better in the future. Circumstances have probably forced you to put away the childhood view, but the adolescent one is equally unrealistic. We may have no tomorrows. Or if we do, life may be *worse* tomorrow. The future makes no promises or guarantees. There are no simple permanent solutions in life.

What do we know with certainty? We know that one egg and one sperm joined, and eventually, at a particular moment, of all the potential persons, a certain, specific child was born. In the explosion into this world comes the miracle of life, the wonder of it all is the central certainty is that "I am." We know, too, with undeniable certainty that life will end. At some particular future moment, this "I" will no longer be in this world. Death alone is the permanent resolution.

Of the intervening period that is my life, I know with certainty that I cannot change the past. It is part of my identity and helps to explain my present life. I know, too, that what is going to happen will be different; it

cannot be the same. I know, then, that life is change.
Life's clock contains one other certainty, another un-
changeable fact of life: I am growing older and so are
you.

Refusal to accept the changing nature of life turns
people inward. Those who do not dare take the risk to
turn outward have a valid fear. They fear that something
worse will happen. Something worse *is* coming—old age.
No matter how well we master, we must face the fact
that age will rob us of many of our personal resources.
The time to learn to strive to put meaning into our lives
is *now* because, inevitably and progressively, our ability
to adjust and to adapt ourselves to the external world
will be impaired.

We all have within us a common trait. We all want to
impose our own desires on others and on the world
around us. Governments regiment society, nations go to
war, and homes are filled with strife because of this
trait. Exaggerated concern about our wants, untamed
imposition of our own desires on others turns us inward
in preoccupation with ourselves. We avoid the outside
world. In this position we view ourselves in a distorted
way—as we would like to be, rather than as we are.
Moreover, we view others with the same distortion.

Our desire to have things the way we would like them
is the reason we all have blind spots. We all want to
avoid unpleasantness. Refusal to accept that we cannot
have what we want in the way we want it, that the world
does not comply with our wishes, and that others will
not allow us to impose our desires on them is the root of
personal anguish. For example, if we refuse to accept
that someone close to us is incapacitated by illness or
old age, we will fail to see his need. Our desire that he
be as he was before will prevent us from accepting the
fact that he is not. His incapacities prevent him from

attempting to impose his desires on us, so his isolation increases. We, in turn, will be frustrated because it is impossible for him to be as we want him to be. Thus, we embroil ourselves in inner conflict.

We must constantly strive throughout life to control this demand for compliance to our wants. Unless we tame it, we will be engaged in a continual battle with reality, unable to have real relationships. Essential to the struggle to control this desire and to accept reality as it is, is the realization that others have the same desire to impose themselves on us. The reciprocity of a real relationship is based on empathy, that is, on an awareness of the needs and feelings of others, and on compromise, the ability to satisfy both within the relationship by searching out and utilizing mutually acceptable ways of achieving that satisfaction.

This process of accepting the unpleasant changes that happen throughout life, thus accepting the reality that we cannot have everything we want, is called "adjustment." The struggle to achieve it is a mourning process. Change brings loss in varying degrees. To go on with living we must accept that loss. We grieve over the loss of what was or over not having what we wanted in all life's unpleasant changes—aging, death, illness, physical impairment, divorce, job loss, moving—the list is endless. Unless we can accept our loss, and control our need to have things as we want them, we will not be able to turn our energies outward and go on with living.

There is truth in the saying "Too old to change." If a lifetime is spent avoiding relationships by turning inward, change does become impossible, not because of age alone but because there are no resources left to change with. Aging diminishes resources at the social, physical, economic, and emotional levels. As our alternatives become more limited, our ability to impose our desires on others also decreases. At the same time we are mourning the loss of our youth. Unless we can accept our losses, we will not be able to maintain the relationships that will give us the support we need. Will we have enough personal resources left?

At the gateway to New York harbor stands the symbol of hope, success, and freedom for millions who search for the good life. The giant lady's inscription reads, "Give me your tired, your poor . . . ," but it should add, "if they are young." Our culture does not revere its elderly. For years society has arbitrarily put people out to pasture at the age of sixty-five. If you have lived that long, you are declared too old to be useful. Looked on as a nonproductive member of a culture that idolizes usefulness, your status changes immediately. In fact, society's values, which are geared to youth and mobility, may even be the values of the elderly person's own family. He has no role—or perhaps a very minor one—left within the family, and he may worry about "being a burden" to them.

Modern medicine and technology have extended life. The numbers of elderly are increasing. Some people are aware that the attitude of "uselessness" is creating many problems, but if you look into the activities for the elderly offered in your community, you are not likely to find opportunities for the retiree to continue as a contributing member of the community. Most communities offer some kind of leisure activity, but often only to limited interest groups.

In marriage, too, roles may change for the elderly person, decreasing his status in his own view. If the woman is younger and still working, she is the breadwinner. If she is at home, she must adjust her activities to include her husband. For lack of enough to do, he may become more involved than ever before in running the house, something she may view as an infringement on her domain. At the same time, both spouses find they need to adjust to day-in and day-out living together for the first time in their lives.

Realistically, money should be accepted as one of the essentials of life. Its presence or absence affects us from the day of birth to the kind of funeral we have. As an elderly person, society will support you at a minimal level. Your savings and pension (if you collect one) may carry you further, but consider the plight of the person who retired in 1965. He may even have planned fairly well, but it is not likely he could have forseen the amount of inflation that has taken place since then. His saved dollar simply isn't going to buy him what he thought it would. Given society's values, this sort of decrease in economic level will further depress the retiree's social standing.

Impairment of personal resources from a physical point of view is obvious. How long can we hide from the mirror? Our skin wrinkles, our hair grows gray. Cosmetics and dyes can only hide it for a while. They won't hide the other signs—our stiffness when we climb out of bed in the morning, the extra effort it takes to do the chores we've been doing all our lives, our fatigue at the end of the day, the added time it takes for cuts and bruises to heal. These things happen gradually, but they happen. Eventually, gnarled knuckles will find it hard to tie shoes or button a dress. So much make-up will only look garish. We will have to face it—these are all "normal" changes; they all happen within the range of good health. Illness can rob us of our physical resources far more drastically.

Our limitations in the social, economic, and physical spheres will affect us emotionally. Retirement itself, which we may view as sudden or premature, will force us to face and adapt to a new situation. Our children will be grown and probably won't live near. Will they see us as a financial or physical burden? Will they care? This will become very important to us. By this point in our lives, we will have already experienced the loss of many friends and relatives, perhaps even our spouse. Our friends are aging, too. What if we become sick? Will anybody be left to care?

Our decreasing resources on the emotional level, our very real fears, can lead to failures in mastering, so that our worries and frustrations find no outlet. What happens then to our self-esteem? If we have never learned that we need others, how do we accept support? If we have never learned to give away, to share ourselves, how are we going to get others to take care of us? If we have always been dependent, how can we make others give us even more? If we have been without the richness of interpersonal relationships, is it too late to strive for meaning in life?

Just as aging is a part of the future that we fear, so is death. The fact that we will grow old is linked to the fact that life is not endless. We are bombarded with death. TV has brought it into our homes as a daily happening; funeral directors advertise their wares; cemeteries vie with one another to lure us into planning for the inevitable. We are overexposed to death's trappings and yet still we do not accept it. We talk in realistic terms to our lawyers in drawing up our wills; life insurance is "big business" and we still make our payments regularly, yet we don't really face death. Instead, we hide behind the overexposure; we fool ourselves with glibness; we disguise death in euphemism—and in doing so we rob ourselves of death's dignity. The trees of the forest, whether struck by lightning, toppled by the axe, or collapsed by disease after a lengthy dying—all die with dignity. Why is it that we cannot accept death as a fact of life? Why is it that we choose instead a "living death" in running from it? Why is it that we, instead of using all our energy to live the only life we have, waste it in a futile attempt to avoid its reality?

We avoid talking of death; we shun those who do talk of it, hoping to avoid unpleasant reality. Consider the plight of the terminally ill. We treat them as untouchable, refusing to support them as they are going through the very difficult process of mourning away the loss of their own lives. When time is so precious to them, we isolate them because we do not want to accept the fact that we are losing them. Moreover, they remind us that we, too, must die.

We isolate the aged in the same way. We put them, like the dying, on a shelf, refusing to let them participate in what is left of life. By isolating them, we deprive them of the opportunity to share at the very time that their adaptability is lessened by their diminishing resources.

Loneliness is worse than death. Death is preferable for many of the aged, much better than the empty, hopeless, painful passage of meaningless days. Thus, the incidence of suicide is greatest among the elderly. It is a way of alleviating intense loneliness and gloom. Death ends the pain of living.

There are compensations for growing older. You can do less and less is expected of you. What is unacceptable at forty-five can be humorous and acceptable at seventy. We do and should excuse eccentricities and peculiarities because of age. Without robbing the elderly of their dignity, we can tolerate and forgive foibles, fussiness, and forgetfulness. Like the dying patient, the elderly person is no less a person than before. Regarding the elderly as children or "old crocks" depreciates them, robbing them of their sense of worth.

True, many elderly people do it to themselves. Accepting the view that they have no further contribution to make, that they are in their "second childhood," they make the gloomy forecasts come true. They use age as an excuse to be as spiteful, as obdurate, or as unkind as they feel, without regard for others.

Our old age, yours and mine, need not be like this if we look at our lives in a realistic way. We will have to continue to strive against our desire to impose our needs on others. And we will eventually have to grieve over the loss of our youth and the diminishing of our resources, but we can prepare for it. By accepting the fact that it is going to happen to us, we can include that time of old age in a simple plan of living. Knowing what we would like to do with that time, while considering what we will not be able to do, gives us a way to handle the future as well as the present to our advantage. As circumstances change, we can always modify our plans. The time between birth and death, however much time it is, is all that we have. Do you want to waste it in gloom and uselessness?

Life is change for better or worse, pleasure or pain. It is lived in a world that promises nothing. All mastering is an attempt to keep ourselves in balance with that world. We look out on the senseless chaos which is the secondary classroom. The pain of reality seems so much more potent than its pleasure. Flood, fire, drought, famine, and disease—all natural disasters—bring so much suffering. Added to these, the chronicle of man's inhumanity —war, genocide, pollution, waste, exploitation, murder, and endless other crimes against himself—seems to approach shrieking insanity. The world appears as a seething, senseless confusion: life in this world means years of compounded misery and sorrow. Can any attempt to balance pain with pleasure succeed?

Pain, sadness, and depreciation—the side of death—seem so much stronger than pleasure, gladness, and appreciation—the side of life. Many people who fear pain happening to them turn inward, away from the world, to avoid being hurt. Building boxes of rigid routine to keep pain at bay, they live in self-centered isolation in hope that brutal reality will not touch them. Their rigidity is an attempt to bring order into the senseless chaos, some meaning into their lives. But their refusal to get involved makes certain the very thing they are trying to avoid—meaningless lives. Working so hard to keep out pain, their rigidity dooms them to an inner death as their avoidance of reality prevents them from participating in life.

We face two pages of an open book. On one side is life, which is change and holds no permanence; on the other is death, which is the only simple, permanent solution. Do I hear you saying that it takes courage to commit suicide? It does not! Suicide is the ultimate avoidance, the most isolated private act there is, a washout of life. What takes real courage and strength is to go on with living.

Life is a striving to accept, to adapt and work to make the living of life better within the chaos. The world is not there to serve us or to give to us; it owes us nothing. Rigidity brought about by avoidance of life puts us on the side of death. But where is life—growth, pleasure, and meaning—in the midst of so much pain? It is there in the chaos. Precisely because of its utter impermanence, the confusion is *flexible*. To master well, to balance ourselves with it, to make any sense out of some portion of it, *we* need to be flexible. The inability to take in pleasure and satisfaction comes from rigidly using too much energy to avoid pain. Putting our energy to work at accepting unpleasantness permits us to be open to the pleasures that will counterbalance pain. We will never be able to bring order to all aspects of life but we can strive to make some sense out of portions of it. Flexibility teaches us to adapt to the chaos and brings involvement, appreciation of life, and pleasure; rigidity teaches fear and ends in defeat by the chaos, bringing self-destructive isolation.

We can find a meaning in life by turning outward to take in the support we need and to give it back again. Every openness, each involvement is a risk. If we take in another and add them on to us, we risk the pain of loss. Accepting the death of someone close to us is very, very difficult, but grief is a part of life. Turned outward we can find support even in sorrow.

Grief is loneliness. The closer the one who died, the greater is our feeling of being alone. Ask any parent who has lost a child how very great this feeling of emptiness is, what agony this loneliness is. Mourning out our loss takes time. During that period what we need most is someone to understand, someone to listen, someone to care. When someone close to us dies, people respond in the immediate crisis, but what happens in the weeks and months after the funeral? We feel we cannot burden others with our pain, while they, not knowing what to say or do, avoid us. If we cannot be open in our grief, as with the rest of our lives, we will remain isolated.

Life is a succession of phoenixes rising from the ashes. We strive to accept and adapt to our losses in order to go on with the new. Is the taking in worth the pain that may follow? If we do not take in life's experiences, we are already isolated and alone. Each taking in adds a new dimension. What the other person gives becomes a part of us. His death can never rob us of the growth and dimension we have gained by involvement with him. Our pain of loss is real and we have to deal with it, and after we have mourned it out and accepted our loss, we adapt anew to start over. The opportunity to start again is the continuation of life.

Involvement with life is a two-way street. Taking in without its counterbalance of giving away leads to the kind of rigidity that seeks only its own pleasure. The inability to give away of oneself indicates that no growth is taking place. If what we take in does not change us by becoming part of us so that we respond in a new dimension, we have not grown. Lack of growth is on the side of death.

In order to participate in life, we need to have flexibility to take in *and* to give away in response. Just as an idea loses nothing by being shared with others, we lose nothing by sharing ourselves. We gain. We create a new opportunity to take in by the response of the other person.

Every openness involves a risk. We risk by taking in and we risk by giving away. We may be confronted by depreciation in response. Our gift may be rejected, but we are left with the satisfaction of knowing that the weakness is in the depreciator. He or she is the one who cannot take in. In search of a positive response, we will turn elsewhere. The depreciator denies the response that will nourish life; moreover, he or she, by refusing to take in our gift takes another step toward isolation.

There is so much in reality that depreciates life that to make our lives meaningful we have to turn to the other side—appreciation. Even religion with its promise of a life after death must look to this life. To depreciate any part of this life by saying that it doesn't matter is folly, for that leads people to turn inward. Real religion is a deep and personal involvement. In all true religion, by whatever name he is called, God is the source of life. Life is *now* for us; to depreciate it is to turn away from its source and make him a god of death. Real religion is a community of life that must extend outward, accepting the reality of the chaos, permitting flexibility, bringing sense to our existence through involvement with the needs of the living.

Life is change for better or for worse. There are no simple permanent solutions. Its wonder, hope, and beauty lie in its limitless potential for growth. The childhood view is that grown-ups have it made; the adolescent thinks the future will be better; the adult, the completed person, accepts that growth is never finished, that the future holds no promises, that real life is a continual adjustment, a striving to make life better.

To truly live we have to get involved, knowing that we will never be all that we might. We take in and give away so that we may grow—each new growth creating possibilities for more improvement. The person who strives for meaning in life knows that life is both pleasure and pain. Mastering with flexibility, continually attempting to find a balance, we know that the value of any routine is to conserve energy for more constructive use. If we had to struggle each morning to get dressed, how would we have the energy to meet the day? The adult knows that each day holds good and bad and that life consists of striving for a balance between the two.

A lifetime of giving and receiving, of enjoying the good in life and adjusting to its mishaps and pains will bring us to old age equipped with enough energy to handle the inevitable stresses of the elderly. We will be able to continue to give warmth and affection to those who are the sources of our own nourishment and pleasure. The qualities of kindness, humor, understanding, and warmth do not tarnish with the passing years nor do they leave us lonely. Rather, these are the qualities that age enhances, that grow with experience, that will give us endurance and enjoyment for the length of our days.

Inner growth *can* be a continuing process. If it keeps on for the whole of life, our faces may wrinkle, our hair grow gray and thin, our joints stiffen, but each day will have meaning. In this way we will remain young, for growth is a sign of youth.

It is happening to us now with each tick of the clock. Our flexibility and adaptability diminish as we grow older. Age is going to limit our options. A better way of living is not going to seek us. We have to seek it ourselves. If you have the feeling that there must be more to life than what you have, why are you waiting? The future holds no promises.

Now is the time to face your weaknesses, to accept them and turn away from past battles with yourself. No one is perfect, nor can anyone expect to be. We can strive to control our need to impose our desires on the world around us and we can learn to master in new ways, bringing our lives into greater balance. Avoiding life, turned inward, our emotional schooling may have never taught us to participate in life. Are *you* trapped in a rigid, negative way of dealing with the world—a way that is preventing you from finding any meaning in life? Are you unable to get involved in the richness of relationships that will provide you with the opportunities to expand your interests and bring some balance into your life?

4 / *Hate and Hermits*

To underline the self-destructiveness of negative mastering and to show its effect on others, I am going to describe first the most potent kind of negative mastering. A form of mastering that goes by many names, in its most obvious form we call it hatred, but bitterness, resentment, and envy are its other faces.

Hatred is the sewerage of human emotion, defiling everything it touches—most particularly the one who hates. It comes in many forms. Hate is irrational, poisonous, and death-dealing, and it can be passed from generation to generation. Back country feuds were built on it. Insidiously, with monumental stupidity, we keep it alive in the kind of prejudice that denies opportunity to one sector of society. Eruptions of hate can tear at the roots of the whole structure of society.

As a social disease, hatred's most blatant form is the kind that sent the Ku Klux Klan rampaging throughout the countryside burning homes and hanging people, or the kind that assigned the Gestapo its horrendous mission of genocide, leaving Germany littered with bones. If you doubt hatred's cunning, look at the callous exploitation of crop-pickers or closed unions; if you doubt its staying power, look at Northern Ireland—year after year the mayhem continues as Protestant and Catholic, Christians all, attempt to annihilate one another.

If we hate one group of people for simply being as they are, we were taught this, too, at our parents knees. Knowingly or not, we assumed their prejudices. Most of us, however, do not actively hate a whole group of people. Through ignorance, or whatever reason, we are afraid of them, so we avoid them. Personal hatred is usually reserved for a single individual. This is the form of hatred that touches us most deeply, so deeply that it becomes woven into the pattern of our emotions. In the end, it can rot our very fiber. As a deep personal revulsion directed against another, hatred is a way of resolving a conflict—a way of mastering that is bent on destruction. If we hate, our wish is to eradicate that other being. We want to see him suffer; we rejoice in his pain.

The deepest, truest, most surging hatred is directed against someone who has great meaning to us. The external force has an overpowering influence. We hope our hatred will protect us from this great power. We act out our inner feelings in ugly deeds in order to destroy that power. We do not realize that we can never win. Hatred is self-destructive. We waste our energies in passionate loathing. It consumes us and all the while we are giving the person at whom our hatred is aimed more power in our own minds. We are left with no energy for positive action. In a sense, the person we hate controls us. If we were to chance upon him in the street, we, not he, must duck into the nearest store to avoid meeting. If we see him in a restaurant, our dinner, not his, is ruined. If we allow its contagion to spread, hatred will permeate our entire being and end in emotional suicide. Eventually, the inner rot it causes will make us outcasts from life itself. The force field of our own decay will keep us hermits locked within ourselves in a sea of poison. Alone like this there is no meaning to life. The chaos is within.

Hatred as a way of mastering is used to protect ourselves from being hurt again. Its purpose is to destroy the relationship which has been so hurtful by inflicting as much pain as possible on the other person in retaliation. While it attempts to destroy the other, in reality it enmeshes the one who hates in the negative side of life. What have these people failed to learn that gives the death side so much power?

Lack of education in interpersonal relationships combined with certain circumstances can lead a person down the path of hatred. Just as children learn from their parents as individuals, they learn from them as members of relationships. The impressions of the parental relationship and the relationship of each parent with the child become the models for the child's own relationships. If there is no real interchange within the primary classroom, a child will not learn what a relationship is. Children raised without this knowledge may find themselves in situations which can result in hatred.

Let us look at a certain family where both parents are inward, self-centered people, pleasant but preoccupied with their private concerns. There is nothing outstandingly negative about this family. To all appearances it is an average middle-class family with three children who do reasonably well in school and who participate in the ordinary childhood activities. Fighting is not a problem. What is lacking is any emotional closeness.

The children in this situation have no feeling of deprivation because they have no standard of comparison. This is the kind of family where all walk their divergent life paths, exchanging superficial commonplaces and shallow pleasantries. As imitators, the children have no model to teach them involvement with others. Although they might feel that no one really cares about them, they will not know what caring really is. The whole family

merely scratches the surface of relationship. Their interchange is that of acquaintanceship. They touch verbally,
but rarely on a deeper level.

A woman raised in a family like this may well be a
pleasant, competent worker, living on her own and having what she views as a good social life. Not knowing
what she is missing, she is likely to view herself as self-
sufficient. She has friendships, but all on the only level
that she knows.

A change in circumstances can lead to hatred. Suppose she meets an exciting, dynamic man who introduces
her to the emotional world. Romance blossoms with
lunchtime walks, intimate dinners, roses and candle-
light. For the first time in her life, she gets completely
involved with another person. She had imitated her
parents' coldness up until the time she met him. With
him she experiences for the first time the uplift in self-
esteem that feeling wanted gives. She invests in him all
her positive feelings. In the newness of the experience
of a close relationship she is very likely to expect to be
the center of all his attention. She will put demands on
his time, and resent it if he has other things to do. She
assumes that she means as much to him as he does to
her. As she starts to pressure him, he is likely to find ex-
cuses for not calling. Eventually, he may tell her it's
over.

How will she react to such a blow? Her deprivation
is enormous. When we are hurt, our first response is
usually anger. In this woman's case, the intensity of her
hurt is likely to produce a blinding rage. There are several ways she may react to protect herself from ever
repeating the experience. Her tendency would be to use
some form of negative mastering and turn inward.

A complete inversion would be a total denial that life
has any meaning at all. In the most extreme ultimate

avoidance, she might commit suicide. A less uncommon reaction would be to avoid ever becoming involved with another man. If she does this to avoid being hurt again, she will project onto all men her feelings about this man. She will assume that all men are a threat. To keep them away from her, she will depreciate them to protect herself. Another reaction would be to become the opposite of what was done to her. Never wanting to be the cause of so much hurt, she could still avoid relationships by sugar-coating everyone with an artificial "I-must-be-kind-at-all-times" attitude. In all these cases, she would ensure for herself a continuation of her past life. She would remain isolated from others, unable to take opportunities, to strive to add on what is missing from her emotional education because she would be making the avoidance of real relationships a way of life.

There is another avenue she can take. She can give her rage free rein. She can nourish her rage by going over and over again what her ex-lover did to her, building it up so that he remains the focus of her attention. This path leads to hatred. If she responds by focusing her formerly positive energy to the negative side, she will give his action too much meaning. If his rejection reactivates in her unpleasant memories of parental rejection, past resentment will add fuel to her pain. She will ascribe even more power to him. To protect herself against the pain and power of that external force, she will hate. Attempts at retaliation will only reinforce her hatred, for she will never be able to hurt her former lover as much as he hurt her. By hatred, she will ensure the very thing she is trying to protect herself against. Her aim is to destroy him in her life, but hatred will keep him alive within her.

People who are rigidly righteous can also use hatred as a way of mastering. For example, suppose a man was overindulged as a child by a possessive mother. She overrode the influences of his apathetic, self-centered father. Nurtured on the idea that his desires were all that mattered, the young man never learned to tolerate delays or positive control of his impulses. He surely did not learn the interchange of the essentials of life. He covers his weaknesses with a wall of righteousness.

A man like this would tend to be authoritative and emotionally distant with an exaggerated view of his own importance. He would have a stern code of behavior to which he rigidly adheres. Moreover, he would expect others to abide by this same code, especially his family. He uses others as a source of his nourishment. Insisting that his family live up to his inflexible and impossible demands, he attempts at all times to remain the center of attention. What is likely to happen should one of his children break his rigid code?

Most parents react with frustration when a child, say their son, gets into trouble with the law for the first time. Although many parents realize that adolescence is a time for exploring, they are likely to feel disappointed and angry at their child's lack of judgment if he carries adolescent experimentation this far. The first reaction of many may be a depreciation: "Why did you do it; how could you be so dumb?" For most parents, this attitude passes as they try to gain some understanding and strive to help their child by meeting his needs as best they can.

But the father who views himself as all-important and has placed his own rigid expectations on his son is liable to react with: "How did you dare to do this to me!" His son's misbehavior is taken as a personal affront. Such a parent is likely to heap depreciation upon punishment in hope of ensuring that the boy will never go against his code again. The father's action swells out of proportion to his son's intention. The father is on hatred's pathway.

Carrying it a step further, this parent may say: "I disown you. You got yourself into this mess; don't come to me. I want nothing further to do with you." The father hates his son and wants to destroy him. This man reacts so strongly because if any attack on his rigid position were to succeed, his inner emptiness would be exposed. He sees his son as having too much power because he broke the paternal code. Without that code, the father is defenseless. He cannot tolerate this threat, which he sees as an attempt to destroy him. He disowns his son in an effort to protect himself.

It is even possible for a rigidly righteous man like this to be pleased with how he deals with his unappreciative children. In the end, such an individual, repetitiously using this way of mastering, will spit out all his relationships. He will prefer to be alone because he will be unable to tolerate anything but a mirror image of himself. Turned inward like this, he is a hermit no matter where he is. The constant use of a single way of dealing with the outside world will eventually trap him within himself.

There are times when we all may be deeply hurt by another. If we nurture our rage, we can find ourselves enmeshed in hatred. If we do not strive to control our anger, our externalized response will be out of all proportion to what provoked it. We will damage our own lives to a greater degree than our malice can hurt another.

There is an element of deliberateness in hatred. It intends to inflict pain for hurt received. We need to examine this question of intent if we are to control our rage. When others hurt us, we need to ask ourselves:

"Was it deliberate? Am I blaming the other too much?"
Just as we cannot blame our parents for not teaching us
what we needed to know because they were ignorant
themselves, we cannot blame others for unintentionally
hurting us. If a person is unaware of the magnitude of
the hurt he has caused, there is no reason for our fury.
When this is the case, allowing our rage to turn to hatred
certainly makes no sense.

You need to look at yourself. If you, for example,
blame your parents for your weaknesses, if you harbor
a resentment against one of them that you cannot shake,
are you sure that you are not nurturing the seed of
hatred? Like it or not, they are a part of you. In resenting them you are resenting a part of yourself. Hatred
of someone else is a sign that he or she has tremendous
meaning for you. To stop the downward spiral that will
lead you to self-destruction, you have to put hatred
aside, otherwise he or she will continue to control you.
Keeping in mind that your parents did not deliberately
set out to leave you incomplete, can't you forgive them
and accept their legacy with the view: This is what I
am. They were the way they were, they did not know
any better. I cannot throw pieces of myself away, but I
can add on and do something about learning to live
another way. If your hatred or deep resentment is directed toward another who has hurt you deeply, chances
are they too did not know any other way of doing things.
They were probably too self-centered to know the effect
they would have on you. Moreover, it doesn't make
sense to waste so much emotional energy on the destructive side when the way to a better life lies in the other
direction. Someone else may have hurt you, but you
don't have to let him or her ruin your life.

Accept what you cannot change and look for another
way. The passage of time lessens the meaning of your

hatred or bitterness. Why keep it alive? It leads only to isolation. A better way is to strive to understand your past feeling as a means of self-protection which you no longer need. Then you can put your energy toward regaining flexibility and openness. By doing this, you mourn away the unpleasant meaning of the past. You can turn back to the side of life with the awareness that past hurts have left you overcautious and fearful of relationships. Your oversensitivity is understandable. Others can accept that in you. It makes no sense not to accept that yourself and then try to bring some meaning into life.

5 / *Pleasure Is My Right*

Our intellectual education is a specialized affair. With increasing complexity of subject matter, with advancement from level to level in school, our teachers focused more and more on their particular fields. Not so with our emotional schooling. Emotional training was left to our parents, who knew only what they had learned from their parents and what they had been able to add on for themselves. Thus, no one has a perfect emotional pattern. No one's parents were perfect. Some merely had fewer, less potent insufficiencies than others.

By focusing the blame on the past, we become bogged down within ourselves, turned inward, missing the meaning of the present, and unable to plan for the future. If we do not come to terms with the parental impressions we see in ourselves, especially those we do not like, we will remain turned inward, never quite able to detach ourselves from the expectation that others are supposed to supply our emotional nourishment.

More pleasure than pain, more gladness than sadness, that is a realistic hope in life. But to have this kind of life, to achieve an inner harmony, we need to be able to balance ourselves with the uneven world outside. We have to be able to activate ourselves to restore harmony when it is threatened. There are periods in all our lives when we

63

must endure worry, fear, pain, or grief, but they do not last forever. If we can master constructively, we will be able to achieve a balance even in the hard times. To do this we have to be able to take in warmth, interest, and affection, and to respond to these qualities with our own warmth, giving comfort back to others. If, however, we cannot do this, we will remain caught in an unfulfilling lifestyle that will leave us with the feeling that life has very little meaning.

There is a group of people who commonly misidentify the essentials of life, or who, by exaggerating one essential, deprive themselves of the others. Among this group are those who have never learned that real satisfaction requires effort on the part of the individual. These are the "I want what I want, when I want it" people of the world. They are trapped on the childhood level of always taking, never giving. They do not hate because nothing has that much meaning for them. All they know and recognize are their own shallow needs and pleasures. Caught in the quicksand of instant gratification, incapable of a close relationship, they see others only as a source of their own pleasure. Their only purpose in giving away of themselves is to keep the process of indulgence going.

There are two major types of takers who believe that pleasure is their right: draculas and parasites. The chief difference between them is that the draculas drain as much as they can from one person and move on to the next; the parasite, however, latches on to an individual and uses helplessness to remain at the center of attention. In the primary classroom they should have learned to absorb the essentials of warmth, interest and affection for their own emotional nourishment and then to give them away to others. The exchange of nourishment is an ongoing process. Instead, all they learned was to take in a misidentification of the essentials of life.

Dracula is often a man who has identified affection and warmth with sexual gratification; who is interested chiefly in himself; and who uses money as a means of getting what he wants. The parasite usually equates the essentials of life with protection and indulgence. Using a woman as an example, she cannot let go of the source of that indulgence. For this reason she has a greater chance than the dracula of eventually learning what she needs to know. If one source stops giving to a dracula, he finds another, but the parasite tends to infect a single host. As her host weakens, her emotional nourishment is threatened and her fear of having to solve her own problems becomes so great that she is forced to face her inabilities and seek help. This will not happen to a dracula unless all the sources of his pleasure have disintegrated. For those involved with him, the only way to help him is to extricate themselves.

Let us look at the dracula first. He is like a plastic man who is fed but can never assimilate his food and use it for growth. Outwardly successful and charming, he will flatter you and promise you the moon, but he'll never deliver. His line often starts with "Where have you been all my life?" If you take him seriously and get involved, he will glibly pass out these gems of flattery for as long as you nourish him. As soon as you put some demand on him, he'll be gone—on to the next "most beautiful."

On first impression, the dracula is a likable man. You probably would feel comfortable with him, perhaps even admire him because he seems so adaptive and flexible. He may be gregarious or good-looking, a peacock with his plumage spread, but he is certainly an exceedingly self-centered man. The typical dracula is unaware that his upbringing deprived him of the opportunity to learn what a relationship is or what empathy is. Usually his primary classroom lacked control and consistency. The parental relationship lacked warmth and outward display of affection, both of which were carried over to the children. At times the atmosphere between the parents may have been outwardly disagreeable, but few draculas retain childhood memories of emotional involvement or upset. Commonly, a dracula views his mother as a selfish woman. Because of the lack of warmth at home in his childhood, he is likely to take on the superficial imitation of his environment, looking to it for acceptance. As an adult, he is as fickle as the wind and exaggeratedly adaptable. He is willing to verbalize his faults to please you, but he is not willing to change.

A common type of dracula is so preoccupied with sex that his descriptions of his exploits make one wonder how he finds time for anything else. Yet financial and social success are often indications to him that he knows everything he is supposed to know. He understands giving away of himself only in terms of monetary generosity.

If we look realistically at the society we live in, money is a key to social status. A common social value—the measure of a person according to how much money he possesses—has some validity because money is *one* of the essentials of a better life. To deny that it is is to deny reality. If you and your family are hungry, the good life is a pipe-dream. Often the dracula's mistake is believing that money is the *only* way to sharing. Thus, his self-achievement is extremely constricted. The kind of marriage he makes is a good gauge for measuring how small his achievement really is.

The dracula tends to marry a motherly type of woman who is too understanding. She tends to take on the burdens of others to an exaggerated degree. The dracula is starving for tenderness and compassion. He demands that she give unceasingly to him and will admit: "I can never be satisfied." The self-pleasure he seeks is so overwhelming that the relationship is engulfed. He always "wants to have his cake and eat it too." He uses her and she lets him do it beyond all ordinary self-respect. She may work while he finishes school, support him through all the years of struggle, and raise the children almost singlehandedly because he is rarely home. He tends to forget the times of struggle, and as they climb up the ladder of success, the marriage deteriorates.

Achievement of business success gives the dracula the feeling that he has it made. His grandiosity percolates into his marriage. With deadly honesty and with no inkling of the effect it might have on her, he is likely to tell his wife of his sexual escapades. He may leave her, or vice versa, but within a short time he will call her, begging her to take him back. He promises and cajoles; she relents. They get back together until he gets bored again. Then the cycle repeats itself.

The dracula's marriage is an extension of his past life. He remains a perennial adolescent. In childhood, he expected others to supply him with emotional nourishment and he does so still. Identifying affection with sex, he sees sexual pleasure as the equivalent of the everyday interchange of tenderness that is a part of a real relationship. He takes his own shallow pleasures with unceasing greed, using everyone with whom he becomes involved. He makes no effort to give away of himself. He is a con artist. While he gets what he wants, he will not change.

His exaggeration of the meaning of sex and his view of women as the source of his pleasure are, in reality, demeaning to all women. By exaggerating his own importance and vaunting his sexual prowess, he is actually trying to prove to himself that he is a man. In reality, he is merely the shell of a man.

How can you deal with a man like this? The only way to stop a dracula is to stop giving to him. The simplest way to protect yourself is not to get involved. He's easy to fend off if you have a sense of humor. Don't take him seriously. Laugh at him and he will turn away. If you don't believe him, he fears that you see his weakness. Moreover, you cannot be a source of his nourishment if you don't take him seriously.

If you are involved with such an individual, you must take yourself away from him. He's not going to change with you; he's using you. Stop the nourishment. By doing this you will have a chance at having a better life —and there is a chance that you will help him. Otherwise you may fall into his trap—give me, give me, give me, but don't expect to receive anything but hurt and neglect in return.

There is a tendency among such men for their inter-personal relationships to change in middle age. Time has a way of changing the meaning of things. The dracula may avoid real involvement with others for a long period of years. By middle age he can review many, many rela-tionships that have no meaning. As future loneliness and isolation threaten, he may realize that he has not even tried to establish a meaningful relationship. What his mirror shows him may stop him from conning himself into believing that pleasure is his right.

Draculas avoid the richness of relationships in one way; parasites do it in another. Parasites, too, use others and are equally incapable of putting effort into life. Like draculas, parasites can never be satisfied, but their method of get-ting what they want is different. Parasites seek out a single host, latch on, and eventually infect the host. Helplessness, submissiveness, and suffering are their way of keeping themselves at the center of attention. They are more than willing to admit their incapacities, for these are the very things that maintain them in their position. They view in-dulgence and protection as the essentials of life.

Constant repetition of this kind of mastering often leads them to the attitude: "I will do nothing. If I don't do anything, no one will rely on me and I will avoid disapproval." For all of us, doing nothing is doing something. By inactivity we force the other person to increase his activity. A simple example: Look at what happens when a person tries to get our attention and we don't respond. What does he do? He calls more loudly, does he not? If we still don't answer he's likely to find himself getting angry and may begin shouting at us. By doing nothing we have caused him to increase his exertions. Thus, the parasite's attitude—"I can't do this. It's too much effort. Help me. Do it for me."—activates others. Parasites are unable to do something positive to help themselves.

What kind of emotional education leaves a person so willing to abdicate? To use a woman as an example, suppose that her father was the central figure in her family. He made all the decisions for everyone in the family, incorrectly assuming that he was satisfying the needs of the entire family. His intention was to make his family happy and secure; he did not know that he was denying them the opportunity to assert themselves. By keeping his daughter dependent on him, solving all her problems for her, extending control into all areas of her life, he neglected to school her to initiative. If his daughter interprets his indulgence and protection as the essentials of life, she is likely to become a parasite. Robed in a false sense of superiority, expecting others to give to her, she is likely to hide her lack of initiative behind a quiet façade. She is likely to assume that if a person cares for her, he will do everything for her. Underneath, she is afraid of asserting herself for fear of disapproval.

A woman like this would tend to marry someone who has the characteristics of determination and assertiveness. With these qualities, combined with her inactivity, he will take over the decision-making process in the relationship. Instead of making up for her weakness, her marriage tends to intensify it. As she becomes less active over time, the emotional carousel will pick up speed. Her increasing helplessness will sap the energy of her husband. Unpleasantness and disapproval will result as his tension and frustration accumulate. Eventually, he will weaken. He may even want to get off the merry-go-round. The very thing she wants to avoid will happen: his weakening will threaten the security she craves. Her fear will increase. The overburdened relationship may snap, but it is probable, precisely because she is so dependent, that a couple like this will seek out help.

To break this kind of cycle both need to understand how they have been affecting one another. The husband needs to learn to give his wife encouragement and support instead of orders. She needs to understand that her life-long demand for instant gratification has left her with a very low tolerance of delay and has deprived her of the self-esteem that only individual achievement can give. A realistic beginning for such a person is a small, short-term task. Like all first steps in learning, it needs to be simple.

When effort and assertiveness are the missing ingredients in the primary classroom, and there is no secondary source from which to learn, people are smothered in fluff and left without substance. Draculas and parasites drain their environment without ever winning real satisfaction, because their growing-up process is incomplete. They cannot activate themselves. Unaware of what they were supposed to know, they expect others to continually nourish them. They do not know that giving nourishment to others is as essential for self-esteem as taking it. Without the self-nourishment gained by giving away the essentials of life, there is little hope of improving the quality of life.

If you hold the principle that "pleasure is my right," you need to learn that true satisfaction is earned. Assess your strengths and accept your weaknesses. You cannot expect to add on overnight what you are missing, nor, knowing your limitations, can you expect to become the opposite of what you are. If you are a drainer, you need to learn to counterbalance your limitation by turning outward and by putting effort into asserting yourself and into the relationships that you have. Realistic appraisal of yourself should tell you that to do this you must start simply. If you take on too large a job, your discouragement will be too great when the going becomes difficult. Just as long division is far beyond the capacities of the small child who can barely count to ten, so, too, in emotional school we cannot ask the impossible of ourselves.

Self-centered pleasure seeking will not bring meaning to life. It will leave you turned inward, avoiding real involvement. You will miss the richness of closeness with others that puts meaning into the passing years. Turned away from others, seeking only what you want, you will never have the pleasure of sharing.

6 / *I Must Be Right*

While those who have not learned effort in the primary classroom seek substance by draining it from others, those who have learned effort and nothing else identify their own performance as the source of self-worth. They do not know how to enjoy themselves.

Our social values also contribute to the making of these people of action who lack the ability to take in emotional essentials. A common social value is that achievement is the most important aspect of life. Performing well, doing things right, and earning enough money to give us status are commonly viewed to be the sources of true satisfaction. The view that work takes precedence over all else in life and that joyless effort is a better way of life than any other are carryovers from a stern and unbending cultural heritage.

The attitude that achievement alone gives meaning to life is a common one. One indication of this emptiness is the number of people who, having achieved their dream of a beautiful home, money in the bank, the right education for their children—all the trappings of the American Dream—look up when they reach 40 and say: "Is this all there is? I've made it. Isn't there any more to life?" They have achieved what they thought they wanted and now they discover that they don't know how to be satisfied.

72

Here again, you can see the exaggeration of one of the essentials of life to the exclusion of others. The man totally preoccupied with money has deprived himself of the other essentials—warmth, interest, and affection. Wealth becomes synonymous with might and right and is seen as the only way to a better life. As the sole goal in life, comfortable as you may be with all the things you possess, money cannot buy you a close relationship, nor can it cure you of disease.

While money is for some all that matters, for others how it is earned is the only standard. The measuring of a person by his work is an attitude which affects our whole culture. We greet someone with the words, "How do you do?" Inwardly, we ask "What do you do?" Our tendency is to describe each other like figures in a nursery rhyme. We answer the question "Who is he?" with *what* he does. "He is a . . . doctor, lawyer, Indian chief, etc." How rarely do we reply: "That is (John). You would enjoy meeting him. He's one of the kindest people I know." Or "That is (Jane). She is interesting, thoughtful, and humorous"—all the various characteristics that truly make us want to know someone.

Considering the prevailing attitudes, we really shouldn't be surprised at how many people equate their identity with how they perform. Poor performance means worthlessness. Limited to this view of themselves, such people are forced to maintain an "I-must-be-right" position, which is their equivalent of performing well. If what they are doing is seen as wrong, they will have nothing left. These are the people who are missing the capacity for pleasure because pleasure is not performance. They go through life with the feeling "I just can't seem to enjoy myself."

This kind of weakness shows itself in several types of people. Perhaps you will see yourself reflected in one of them. They are the Mr. Perfects, the burden bearers, the wallflowers, and the martyrs. All are aloof, rigid people, who are oversensitive to criticism, inwardly frightened, and unable to express their feelings. All are overly fearful of disapproval. All are limited to performance as the only means of attracting the relationships they desire and have never learned to extend themselves to other people. It is in their use of performance that they differ. Mr. Perfect's attitude is "my way is the only way." The wallflower is aware of her fear of being wrong and uses what she does as a way of proving that she is right: "I am doing this, so I must be good." The martyr's attitude is: "See how hard I work for you, how much I do and endure; I am better than you." Let us examine these ways of mastering more closely.

Cautious, conscientious, and critical, concerned with the smallest detail, Mr. Perfect is hard to like although he has many assets. He is thoroughly reliable, highly moral, determined, sincere, and diligent. He takes his obligations seriously, and we admire him for these qualities, but he exaggerates them. Aloof instead of friendly, and cold and unaffectionate, he seems to stand alone, apparently uninterested in others. He may laugh with us at our mistakes, but he cannot laugh at himself. He cannot accept criticism nor can he blame himself for error —it's always someone else's fault. On the other hand, he always seems to find our mistakes and zeroes in on them, blowing them up out of all proportion. If we do offer him friendship, his fault-finding will eventually make us turn away. He seems to spit out the overture, at the same time asking us to applaud him. He does not know how to have a close relationship although he does want one. He has never learned how to take in warmth, interest, and affection, nor how to give them away.

Mr. Perfect single-mindedly pursues perfect performance because what he learned was: "If I do it right, I will get affection." His self-esteem depends on correctness. Viewing his way as the right way, he must maintain his position. He would have nothing if he were to accept criticism or were to criticize himself. He has limited himself to performance as his only means of attracting the close relationship he desires. However, his needs to keep his performance untarnished, to see himself as blameless, and to remove any possible threat to his self-esteem make him unable to express his feelings.

This is what his parents knew and, stressing obedience, this was all they were able to teach him. His emotional schooling was restricted to learning that approval could be gained only by a good performance. Consequently, Mr. Perfect is afraid to take in affection because he fears having to do something in response, and he does not know how to make that response. He is afraid to externalize his feelings because he assumes that he will be rebuffed. He wants closeness but makes others pull away, leaving him special and alone.

Mr. Perfect tends to marry a woman who either lives within a similar code (Mrs. Perfect), or who tends to be submissive and dependent. In either case, the code controls his family. The process repeats itself. His children grow up in the same kind of atmosphere as he grew up in. An "I-am-never-wrong" kind of father, he insists on adherence to his standards. "Do it because I say so" is his only method of approach. His children learn from him to avoid taking risks. "If you can't do it right, don't do it," teaches them that they are not allowed to make mistakes. Thus, Mr. Perfect's deficiency is passed on to his children.

The "I-must-be-right" attitude can also be seen in those who unendingly take on other people's problems.

As sensitive to criticism as the Mr. Perfects and afraid to be wrong, they are drawn to others with worse problems than their own. In this way they can view themselves as needed and strong. By comparison they maintain their position. Always giving in the relationship, they never seem to be getting anything in return.

Such a person's need to continually prove to him or herself that "I am good" shows itself in many ways. Some do it with kindness. Having taken on, usually from religious parents, the idea that being kind or doing something for someone else is always right and that saying no or getting angry when someone hurts you is always wrong, these virtuous people are caught in Mr. Perfect's bind. No matter what unreasonable demands are placed on them, no matter what someone does to them, they must return understanding and aid. A good example of this type is the dracula's wife. These are the people who allow themselves to be used by others. They have never learned that at times the real kindness to yourself and to another is to say no. Is it any kindness to permit the dracula to go on and on? By not stopping him you are acknowledging that it is all right for him to use you. It certainly is no kindness for parents to do everything for their children, never showing them that children can make their parents angry. Exaggerated giving to children will deprive them of the opportunity to learn how to give.

Consider the wife and mother who cannot say no to a volunteer cause. What is she really doing to herself when the tenth good cause asks her to canvass the neighborhood while her housework goes undone and fatigue makes her irritable with her family? Deep down she probably has a "why-does-it-always-have-to-be-me?" feeling, resents that she's neglecting her other concerns, feels that she's being used, and yet her fear of appearing selfish keeps her tramping the streets. Saying no would damage her image of herself. She must be "kind." To her, refusal to do something is selfish and bad. Her opinion of herself depends on the approval of others just as it used to depend on her parents' approval. Her exaggerated kindness prevents her from taking in the nourishment that would replenish her supply of energy. She is left with a feeling of emptiness.

Wallflowers are people who have been schooled in family environments that allowed no errors. They had been constantly told that they were wrong and attempted to counter that belief by finding situations that proved them right. Underneath their shyness is a warmth and concern for others that they dare not show for fear of being rebuffed for having done something wrong. Because of this they tend to rely on their work for self-esteem and are devoted to it, but need tangible proof that it is well done. For example, at work they are much more likely to believe raises not praises. Good listeners, they tend to be drawn to people with greater problems than their own because in this kind of relationship they can bolster their fragile self-esteem by comparison.

Overly kind or shy people are not the only ones who too willingly accept the burdens of others. The martyrs of the world also do this, but they give the impression that they do not want our help while they tell us about their problems in dreary detail. They seem almost to enjoy what they endure. At the same time, they say: "If it weren't for you, I wouldn't have to do this. I'm only doing it because it is my duty." They do everything to maintain the relationship with themselves in control. Martyrs are usually raised in rigid, chilly family at-

mospheres. Obligations at home keep such children
limited in their outside involvements. Most times they
miss the ordinary excitements and fun of peer activities,
which might make up for the lack of warmth at home.

Unaware of what they have missed, martyrs often
marry people who seem the antithesis of the tyrannical
parent of their childhood. In doing this they are liable
to choose ineffective people who enjoy, and even insist
upon, being cared for. The spouse's dependence puts
the martyr in a controlling position and continually
proves to the martyr that he or she is right.

This kind of relationship has nowhere to go but down.
For example, take a woman whose father was the tyrant
in her background and who is now married to an alcoholic husband. While berating and threatening, com-
plaining and bemoaning her fate, she stays on year
after year. She begs; he promises. She believes; he
comes home drunk the next day. She threatens; he
drinks more. She picks him up at bars, brings him home,
cleans him up, and puts him to bed, sobering him up so
that he can start all over again. She seems to drink, fig-
uratively, along with him. Eventually, as the downward
spiral continues, she may realize that he has become un-
manageable and just as despotic in his own way as her
father was. Often she decides at this point to divorce
her husband, feeling that he is ungrateful. With the
"after-all-I've done" attitude, she still does not understand her contribution to the situation. By tolerating and
excusing her behavior, by continually taking all those
years of pain and problems, responding always by "bear-
ing up," never expressing her own feelings, she remained in the primary classroom along with him. Her
need to control him backfired. Trapped in the same
"little boy" situation that kept him from learning how
to tolerate his own fears, he used alcohol to make his

inner pain more bearable. When she finally began to pressure him, it was too late. Her threats were simply further proof to him that he couldn't do anything right; her tirades simply provided another reason to drink more: to drown her out.

Limiting life's essentials to wealth or performance, always demanding from yourself proof that you are right, being better than the next person, being oversensitive to criticism, fearing to express your feelings— these do not do much for the quality of life, do they? Hiding behind activity so that you do not have to face yourself is no way to win the satisfaction you want and need.

I have described the major ways that the inability to take in warmth, interest, and affection shows itself. Have you seen yourself here? Do you find it hard, if not impossible to really enjoy yourself? Do you have the feeling that there is no way out? Not so. Understanding and awareness are the first step. If you have recognized yourself, don't you think it's about time to move out of the primary classroom? Can *you* take the step?

7 / I Can Change Myself

Rainbows, those brief flashes of enchanting beauty, vanish quickly, leaving us touched with promise, hope, and wonderment. Rainbows that last forever, Christmas magic every day, happiness every minute—these are visions, the impossible dreams that won't come true. Life simply is not like that. Nor will it ever be. Frustrations, disappointments, tensions, problems, pains, and sorrows are unavoidable. They will happen, but they need not be all, or even most, of life. What we can achieve is a better balance: gladness can outweigh sadness, times of pleasure can see us through the periods of pain, moments of success can balance the failure. This is the better life.

But we have to accept what we cannot change. If something happened yesterday, we cannot undo it, but we need not let it drain us. Moreover, there are some unpleasant facts we need to accept about the future. Not wanting to grow old or wishing that there were no death will not stop them from happening. Since both are unavoidable, is it realistic to refuse to face them?

We cannot enjoy everything that happens from day to day. We all have things we must do which we do not like. Housecleaning is a fine example of a necessary task that is unpleasant for a great many people. Some loathe it so much that they live in a disorganized mess that is not

only unsanitary but gives their homes a depressing atmosphere. Wasted energy and resentment abound as
someone tries to find a needed item that is hidden at the
bottom of cupboard chaos. How much more constructive
it is to simply accept the fact that housecleaning must be
done. We should stop wasting our personal resources in
resentment that will spill over into other areas of our lives,
and go ahead and do the work. Doing what must be
done will release us to enjoy what we would *like* to do
without robbing ourselves of fun by feeling that we
should be doing something else.

No one enjoys the pains and problems of life, but too
often energies are dissipated, sapped by resentment
and blame. The "why-did-it-have-to-happen-to-me?"
battle exhausts our internal forces and reminds me of
the "why-is-the-sky-blue?" kinds of childish questions.
What possible improvement can this outlook bring to
any situation? If you are locked into this approach, it is a
sign that you have learned too well the negative mastering of avoidance or that you are limited to a single mode
of mastering that cannot be applied to all the circumstances in which you find yourself. For example, the person whose only release for emotional tension is activity,
whose sense of self-esteem depends on viewing himself
as independent, is in a fix if he gets ill or breaks a leg.
His depression and irascibility only make matters worse.
If the prognosis for full recovery is good, he tends to
waste his convalescence instead of using the time constructively. If recovery is not possible, or will be less
than complete, his discouragement increases. All of us
find that adjustment to physical limitation difficult, but
he, confined as he is to a singular mode of release, may
never be able to adapt. He needs to find constructive
uses for his energy.

What if the uncomfortable circumstance in which you

find yourself is your fault? You have made a mistake, failed at something, and are trapped in its consequences? Should you blame yourself, ignore it, or find others to blame? Certainly self-flagellation is no nourishment for your self-esteem. No one deliberately sets out to make himself miserable. All mastering is an attempt to gain inner satisfaction. You have tried, but you have failed. Why not look at it this way: "I am not, nor can I be, perfect. I made a mistake. It is done and I cannot undo it." Acknowledge the portion of the blame that belongs to you—but don't stop there. Consider whether, given the circumstances, there is something you can do to correct the condition. If there is, do it. If not, put it aside; you have gained the knowledge of what not to do again. In trying to make amends, by forgiving yourself and acquiring new knowledge you will have put failure to its best possible use. By approaching our mistakes and failures this way, we can take a destructive thing and turn it around.

Let's take a look at blame from the point of view of someone else. Suppose you are being criticized. Evaluate the criticism. Is it appropriate or not? Does it belong to you? If you are to blame, acknowledge it. If only part of the blame is yours, take the percentage that belongs, admit it, and put the other aside. If the other person wants to continue to accuse you, there is nothing you can do. If that's the way he wants to think, it is not your problem; it is his. You will not be able to change his thinking even if it is possible to correct your error.

A simple example of this is the case of being shortchanged by a cashier. If I catch him in the act and point it out to him, he will probably say, "You're right. I'm sorry. I miscalculated." He will then give me the correct change. He has admitted his error and amended it. If I continue to suspect him of having done it deliberately and choose to judge him dishonest, there is absolutely nothing he can do to change my mind. It is my choice to believe him or not; he cannot control it.

Our inner world is like the outer. Just as there are inescapable unpleasant realities outside us, there are unavoidable limitations within. Identification and awareness of our weaknesses are not enough. We have to accept them. Until we do, we will be unable to consider what alternatives are open for improving them. The alcoholic who refuses to accept the fact that he has had too much to drink will go right on drinking.

Likewise, if you are impatient you are certainly not going to change for the better if you constantly blame another for what you view as their procrastination. Procrastination is *their* problem, which you cannot control. You need to be aware of *your* fault and admit to it. Your impatience is not going to vanish by magic. There will always be times when it will show itself even if you do learn how to wait for most things. When it does show and you are criticized for it, if you openly acknowledge it, you are doing two things: accepting appropriate blame by admitting to yourself and another that you are not, nor can you be expected to be, perfect; and showing your strength, which is your ability to be open with others by exposing your weakness.

Identifying and understanding the problem is the first step. Accepting your weakness is the second. This is good, and you are on the right road, but it is not sufficient for effecting a change. Shouting your weaknesses from the rooftops will not stop you from behaving in the same way nor will it change your way of mastering. You need to negotiate with yourself. Only you can assess the hurt you are doing to yourself and to others, and the benefits that will accrue to you and others if you really do change. To establish the pros and cons, to weigh the value of each side in any negotiation with yourself, I recommend using a paper and pencil. Tangibly seeing the possible alternatives and their consequences before you will help you in assessing the importance you attach to each of them. The ability to assess alternatives and to negotiate well helps self-growth because it permits flexibility. The capacity for negotiation with others nourishes compromise, which is necessary for establishing close relationships and for giving these relationships longevity.

Let me illustrate what I have been saying. Some people become anxious when they meet a new group of people. They worry because they just can't seem to start a conversation. They don't know what to say and are afraid of saying the wrong thing. Most people feel some anxiousness about new people or new situations, but some people seem able to relax more easily. Suppose that this is a difficulty for you and that it shows itself especially in social situations. You need to examine what you usually do. Do you find a corner, stay for as long as is polite, and drink too much to relax yourself?

Whatever it is you do, if you want to change it, consider the alternatives. What would happen if you did go up to that group of people and introduce yourself? Should you go or shouldn't you? On the pro side the possibilities are: you might meet some interesting people; you might learn something; you're sure to enjoy yourself more, because you're uncomfortable now standing alone. On the negative side: you're afraid to do it because they may shut you out; you might get hurt.

At this point, many find it hard to carry their self-negotiation any further. The next step is to weigh the importance of the factors involved. Your reasoning might go like this: I am afraid because I *might* get hurt, but I'm already uncomfortable standing here pretending to look occupied. What have I got to lose since I'm already hurting? If you decide to take the risk, you must test your solution: Am I hurting myself or someone else by doing this? In this case, since the choice is between a situation which is already hurtful to you and one which involves perfectly acceptable behavior, the solution passes the test.

In this process, I have understood, accepted, negotiated, determined, and tested my choice, and now I am ready for the final step—to actually do it. *I have to activate myself.* I need to turn outward and do something in order to improve my situation. If I do nothing, I had better be willing to accept the consequences. My unenjoyable evening is my own fault because I have not even attempted to improve it.

If, however, I do make the effort, do take the risk and carry out my solution, I have taken that first simple step toward conquering my shyness. I will never be the life-of-the-party type—that's simply not me—but rewarded with an enjoyable evening and the satisfaction that comes from activating myself, I will be able to overcome my shyness again. Eventually I will be able to make this new way of doing things a part of me and will counterbalance my reserve by being more outgoing.

Because of the importance of testing the hurtfulness of your decision, you ought to examine this step toward self-improvement in some detail. You must keep in mind that you cannot control another's feelings and thus are not responsible for them if you have not deliberately put the other person in a situation which is bound to be harmful. If, however, what you do creates a hurtful situation, you are responsible for the pain you cause. For instance, if I hate my job, the decision to change it will obviously benefit me, but if I quit without having planned ahead, I am placing my family and myself in a situation that is likely to be harmful. I am responsible for doing that to them. If, however, I have planned and saved, but decide I should stay where I am because my wife might worry or be disappointed or angry, I am not being realistic. It is grandiose to presume to predict another's feelings. In a sense you are telling him how to feel, and that is more influence than anyone should have.

In our hypothetical problem of changing jobs, the natural thing would be for me to talk it over with my wife. In a sound relationship, my satisfaction is her concern, too. Bringing the question out of myself to another, particularly one who is involved in the consequences of its solution, serves two purposes: first, her perspective may provide me with alternatives that hadn't occurred to me; and, second, her interest is an encouragement to reach a decision and implement it. By her responses, be they positive or negative, I will have added a new view to the question. In reality, I am making use of the resources available to me to help myself. Thus, just as I cannot make people feel happy if they refuse to enjoy themselves, I am not responsible for their feelings of sadness and pain if I have not done an intrinsically hurtful thing. Their feelings belong to them, not to me.

Sometimes our choice lies between two hurtful situations. Suppose a wife discovers her husband is having an affair. Should she pretend she doesn't know and by her silence allow it to continue? By doing this she is acknowledging that the affair is all right with her and is thus responsible herself for the increasing pain it will cause. By doing nothing she is hurting herself and is thus adding to the hurt her husband is causing. In contrast, consider the question of whether an unfaithful spouse should tell the other about an affair. I call this "deadly honesty." The only purpose it serves is to destroy the relationship.

The unfaithful spouse is responsible for the guilt he or she feels; it is the deserved consequence of something done alone. It gives no license to inflict pain on another.

Problem, acceptance, negotiation, decision, and testing must be followed by activation. If we cannot decide, constantly sitting on the fence and turning back to renegotiate, our acceptance is incomplete. There is the feeling "I know what I should do, but I just can't make myself do it." This last step is critical. If putting off decisions is your lifestyle, you are not an activator.

Activation is not merely understanding. Nor are activators merely reactors or provokers, forcing others to supply their needs. Activators are able to take in and to give away in a reciprocity that enables them to keep the process of living turned toward the positive side. Aware of the realities of life, they are flexible and adaptable. Able to enjoy themselves and to give enjoyment to others, they master well. This ability to do something themselves, this self-activation, is the sign and reason of a whole person.

Activation is essentially creativity. It is an original outgoing movement, the expression of an internal response that bears that mark of uniqueness of the individual. Stamped with the mark "I," activation is an upward, constructive movement that impinges on the external world, seeking a response.

We usually think of the arts as creative and for good reason. If the composer listens only to the sound within his head and never plays it, if the writer never puts his thoughts on paper, or if the artist never paints the picture in his mind's eye, there is no music, literature, or art. When he does create, the artist takes what is inside himself and externalizes it. He has made an expression of himself. Seeing new things, gaining new wisdom, or hearing a different sound, the taking-in from the world around him will strike that creative chord in him and lead him to express himself.

Is the artist truly satisfied with what he has done? He has the satisfaction of "I made it," but is it enough? The day he stops taking in, or the day that he looks at his work and feels it is a "perfect" expression of himself, that is the day he will stop creating.

Is the creative process completed when the artist ceases his work? Unheard music, unseen art, a ballet never danced or a book never read—without an audience all are unfinished. True creativity seeks a response. Anyone who has never been enthralled by a fine painting, a Shakespearean sonnet, or a majestic symphony can give that response and know the creative emotional experience. The taking in from the outside world, the internal response you have, that feeling that is yours alone, these are signs that your own creative chord has been struck.

In the emotional sphere, when the activator takes in and responds internally, he must externalize his response, taking it outside himself. Like the sculptor with his stone, he takes his life and fashions it, so that the whole is marked with his uniqueness. He, like the artist, seeks a response, an answer from the outside world, so that he may take in again, respond again, and activate more and more in an ongoing process of inner growth that continues until death.

Sometimes that response to the activator is depreciation. Breaking down without building up in its place, depreciation is a sign of a machinelike individual, who, having no creativity himself, envies activators. Because of his inability and envy, he cannot admire those who can and do turn outward. The depreciator is attempting to stop the growth of the other. Underneath, the depreciator knows that the one who can activate will eventually outgrow the relationship. Depreciators are often mistakenly seen as strong people. In reality, they are weak, frightened people who tear down because they themselves do not have the very qualities they are depreciating.

There is in the activator a striving to balance all the essentials of life. The activator uses this creative, outgoing movement to take in and give away all the essentials—warmth, interest, affection, and money. A balance of these four is necessary for every one of us who seeks a meaningful life.

Warmth, as we take it in, is the feeling of closeness, comfort, protection, and inner security. As we give it away, warmth is caring for others with tolerance of their limitations, humor, and patience. Warmth laughs and cries with true compassion. It is enjoying ourselves and others, and a returning of that enjoyment to them.

Interest is openness. Within us it is self-honesty, an awareness of our needs and limitations. It takes the risk of letting in the outside world, learning something new and adding it on to ourselves. We give interest back by becoming involved, committing ourselves, and showing our true feelings.

Affection is, in a sense, the "how" of warmth and interest. It is tenderness and kindness. It is taking in the pleasure that others give us and giving it away with the feeling that "my pleasure is pleasing you." We show it in countless ways—a smile, a touch, an offer of aid. It is the kind of feeling that is at once gift-giving and gift-receiving. A compliment, for example, is a sign of affection. A sincere compliment is given because someone has pleased you. It is a way of giving back the pleasure he or she has given us, a way of saying "thank you." Not accepting it, by depreciating it because one feels it is undeserved, is a refusal to accept the gift. The proper response to any gift is "thank you"—not "I don't deserve it." The latter robs the giver of his pleasure in pleasing us. It shows a lack of understanding and appreciation for one of the essentials of life.

It may surprise you that I have included money among the essentials of life. Unlike warmth, interest, and affection, it is tangible. The influence of money on an individual's personality is as real as the fact that he needs food to eat. We professionals are to blame for avoiding this issue. We have looked at environment, inherited characteristics, organic deficiencies, emotional deprivation and have failed to take into account the importance of the presence or absence of an adequate supply of money.

A friendly family atmosphere can go a long way and is the most important factor in bringing up children. With that, but without enough money, we are extremely limited in the alternatives we have in making a decision to improve the quality of life in our homes. Our children will be held back by the narrowness of the exposure we can give them. Moreover, money is the passport into the secondary classroom and the means of proving ourselves away from home. It even determines how we are going to be buried. To avoid talking about it or accepting its influence on our lives is ridiculous.

As with the other essentials of life, the importance of money can be exaggerated. The exaggeration causes deprivation of the other essentials. The purpose of money is to be used, saved, and spent to meet our material needs. Excessive hoarding, the need to have so much all for ourselves, is the same as doing nothing in the emotional sphere. Something important has not been done. Overgenerosity with money to the point of deprivation of ourselves or our family is not a common failing, but overspending on ourselves is. We often waste money by not putting it to its best use. I do not mean the kind of spending that gives us all enjoyment. I am speaking of ridiculous and unnecessary extravagances, the $100 dinner for two. The person who uses money in this way is trying to impress others with his own importance and is usually unaware of the weakness he is showing.

Overgenerosity to our children is like being overly kind. By giving them too much we deprive them of the chance to learn the value of money—how to earn it and how to use it—in much the same way that never scolding them prevents them from learning how they should behave.

The need for money both controls creativity and is a motivation to be creative in getting it. To take the example of artistic creativity once again, the writer may be satisfied with his finished manuscript, but misses a great deal if it is never published. If, however, his work is accepted for publication, his creativity becomes controlled. He will rewrite until his editor is satisfied that his work will sell. Musical instruments, paper, or paint must be acquired for the artist to exercise his talent. Often he must work at another job to earn enough money, thus limiting the time he can spend on original work.

In the emotional sphere, the activator, too, has to meet his material needs. The need for money limits his alternatives. At the same time, it is possible for the activator to be creative about earning enough. If the opportunities are not available, he must make some compromise with himself in order to balance his life. Enjoying his work may not be first on the list of his priorities. Satisfying or not, his work will reward him with money. With this he also earns respectability in our society. Enjoying his work might bring greater satisfaction. While this enjoyment is not always possible, the upward spiral of true activation leads to both monetary rewards for work as well as increased pleasure in doing it.

Understanding of the problem, acceptance, negotiation of the alternatives, decision, testing the decision, and implementation of it—all are necessary. Can you do it or do you find yourself going back, renegotiating, never getting started at improving your life? The need to renegotiate is one sign that acceptance is not complete. If this book describes how you behave in some areas, you have to face the fact that you are not an activator in those areas. If the inability to activate to improve yourself is characteristic of you, it is an indication that you are still caught in the primary classroom. You must still make the emotional separation that lands you with both feet squarely in the secondary classroom of society, able to utilize it, drawing from its resources to add on what you have failed to learn. If you are not an activator, if you cannot help yourself, you have not truly faced yourself.

The infant I described in chapter two actively did something himself to attempt to restore his balance with the outside world: he put his hand to his mouth. As an infant, you undoubtedly did the same thing. Thus, the creative movement from inside to outside is in us all at the beginning of life. It is evident in all children's pleasure when they have done something by themselves. "Look, Mommy! Look what I did!" This movement is there in you. If you cannot activate now, it is a sure sign that the growing process is unfinished, your adult life remains an extension of your childhood. You saw examples of this in the marriages of some of the people I described in preceding chapters.

What happened to those small beginnings? They have

slept there within you, undeveloped, lying unused behind repetitious, complex negative mastering, which you use to camouflage your weakness, hiding the fact that you do not know what you're supposed to know. These small beginnings remained at the childhool level. Like the small child, you are still dependent on others to satisfy your needs. You have never severed the emotional umbilical cord. Your acceptance of the impressions you received is not total. Resenting these impressions, you resent yourself. If you cannot accept the adverse side of yourself, life will be nothing but an inner battle. Rejection of these impressions means rejection of yourself, and this attitude results in nothingness.

How do we emotionally separate from the primary classroom? This book cannot do it for you; it can only show you that it needs to be done and that there are resources available to help you. *Only you can do it.* Admit that you have not completed the circle that will give you inner wholeness and start negotiating with yourself. Remember that the constant need to renegotiate is a sign that real acceptance is lacking. Additionally, keep in mind that adolescence, which is the usual time for making the separation, is a period of years. It doesn't happen all at once, as if by magic. It takes time and effort to overcome the patterns of a lifetime. We need not dwell on unpleasant memories. We can lessen their importance by trying to understand their meaning for us now. Those that began to improve their way of life started simply with small achievable goals.

If you do try to separate emotionally from your parents and are unable, or if your current situation is making this too difficult, or if your discouragement or fears or entrenchment in the primary classroom are too great, you may need professional help. Admitting that you do need help and seeking it is in itself an activation. If you are like this, why wait? It is likely to become more difficult to seek the help you need as the years reinforce your negative ways of dealing with the only life you have. Time is ticking away. . . .

8 / Me and My Children

Understanding the impact of parental impressions on children, who learn by imitation, and aware that we cannot teach what we do not know, we should now examine some of the factors that are most often excluded, or mishandled, in teaching a child to be a person. I do this for those who have not been able to make the separation from the primary classroom to understand what they failed to learn, and for those who have completed the circle and become whole persons, to help them offer their children a more complete education. Our children are the resources of the future. Our greatest hope is that along with physical adulthood they may achieve full personhood, which will enable them to face the pleasant and the unpleasant with strength and maturity, able to make for themselves better lives. This is the purpose of parenthood and our children's finest legacy.

Seeking pleasure and trying to avoid pain are human characteristics. Instant gratification is the infant's way of dealing with the world around him. As he becomes more aware of reality, his needs become more complicated. In order for him to live in the real world, he must learn to tolerate delay and to actively do something to satisfy his needs. He must learn, too, how to handle the unavoidable frustrations and disappointments that await him.

Too often the primary classroom fails to prepare children for living in the secondary classroom. Unable to *separate* and to become activators, they continue to live with their childish notions in the confines of their pasts.

The separation process usually takes place in adolescence, a time of crisis and pain for both parents and children. Why is it so painful? I believe that adolescence is a period of such turmoil because it is basically a time of mourning. When someone we love dies, we grieve. We must complete our mourning before we are able to activate ourselves again to go on with involvement in life. We have the feeling that we must pick up the scattered pieces of our lives and put them back together again. In grief we need to talk and talk about the way it used to be. Over and over again, we go over our loss, wearing it down as a way of softening our pain. This is why in grief we need most someone to listen to us. The mourning process brings gradual acceptance of our loss.

Perhaps resentful and angry at first, we then go on to a period of solitary sadness. If we stay on that level and never find a way to express our feelings, if there is no one to care enough to listen and understand, it is very, very difficult to bring the mourning process to an end with acceptance. Until it is completed, we feel that we are not really living. The sorrow and loneliness within us are too great for us to turn outward. When we have finished grieving—and this takes time—we reactivate ourselves and go on in a different way. Sorrow and sadness can be tolerated. We can reactivate ourselves despite them, but only when we have completed the mourning process. Our loss can never be undone; the sadness will remain to come flooding back with memory, but it can be accepted. We have lost something, yet we can continue in another dimension gaining other things.

The separation process is similar. Seeing themselves

for the first time, adolescents must also face their parents as they really are. This marks, in a sense, the death of their childhood view of their parents as omnipotent—powerful sources of everything children need, sources of security and protection in an uncertain world. Here, too, anger and resentment at their loss may come spilling out. By turning inward, adolescents mourn the loss of what used to be, namely, the passing of their safe, secure world, and they are frightened of the unknown future before them. If they cannot complete the process and accept the loss of childhood, if they stay focused on the past in anger and resentment, the circle is never completed. They cannot take the step that closes the circle, and try to be whole persons.

Preparation for the step out of the primary into the secondary classroom is the whole process of being a parent. Parenthood for us all is the adding on of a new dimension. The birth of our first child is the beginning. That first miracle of life is an enormous occasion that leaves us staggered. Suddenly work and money mean a different thing. A wife is no longer simply that. She is a mother, and her husband, a father. It is elating and more than a little frightening. We have never experienced this before and *we don't know what to do.*

People *learn* to be parents. We all fumble and bumble with our firstborn. We relax a bit with the second—we have been through it before. In his or her uniqueness, each child will teach us different things. What is good for one is not always good for another; they teach us that by the way they respond to us. That feedback is at once our reward and our way of knowing when we are doing something wrong.

The greatest pleasure of loving parents is seeing their children develop. When the parenthood is completed, the children are able to strive for meaning in life. It is from each parent *and* the relationship children witness between their parents that the art of living and loving is learned. The parental relationship is the model by which children learn what a relationship is, in the same way as they receive imitation-impressions from each parent individually. The parental relationship creates the atmosphere of the home. Whatever is happening in it spills over onto the children and becomes the pattern by which they learn to make their own relationships.

For a child to learn to master constructively, there are two basic feelings he must have. It is essential that he have the impressions "I am lovable" and "I can do it." Doubt about, or lack of, these feelings will leave him overfearful of disapproval and afraid to take the risk to be open. If parents habitually give him all he wants, he will never learn "I can do it." If too much emphasis is placed on prohibitions and he fails to feel that he can win parental approval, he will doubt that he is lovable. If parents limit their teaching to a "you-must (or-must-not)-do-it-because-I-say-so" attitude, thus refusing to allow interchange, children cannot satisfactorily learn to take in and give away. From the beginning we must nurture their active participation in their own lives. But the steps we take have to be appropriate for the age and understanding of the particular child. Unrealistic expectations will defeat your purpose just as thoroughly as no expectations at all.

In the process of preparing children for separation from us by teaching them to master the reality of the outside world, we cannot omit teaching them how to handle life's unavoidable hurts, frustrations, and failures. If they cannot tolerate unpleasantness, there is little hope that they will complete the process of mourning that marks maturity.

How often do parents simply say to their children, "I

made a mistake?" Even "I don't know" is hard for some parents to admit to their children. Instead, they are much more inclined to say "You're too young to understand," or "I'm upset," or "It's not your concern," or "It's just one of those things," without explaining that "one of those things" is "I made a mistake." From a child's point of view, his parents are perfect. Eventually, he will discover that they have failed in some way. Seeing failures, but never hearing an admission of failure, he learns only that he should hide failures and weakness. How much better it is for him to learn that everyone, including his parents, makes mistakes. If he sees you do something wrong, admit it and cheerfully do the task over again; he will see how to handle his own mistakes, an invaluable lesson for the future.

Similarly, how often do you hear parents apologize to their children? A simple "I'm sorry" not only shows them that you can admit the weakness that is in you, but that the consequences of what we do affect others. Children will learn to make up the hurts they cause others. In this kind of interchange, there are added dividends. Apologizing to your children is an affirmation by you that they are persons, too, that you respect them and are truly concerned about them. Moreover, you are helping them to develop an essential feeling that they can use in all relationships throughout their lives. Apologizing will teach them the forgiveness that will enable them to tolerate the limitations of others.

Parental approval is the source of children's sense of self-worth. In all areas, the common courtesies that we accord others—"Please," "Thank you," "You're welcome," "I'm glad to see you," etc.—go a long way toward giving them that sense. Children see and hear you treat others that way, why not them?

We have spoken of the beginnings of creativity, which

is the key to enjoyment. So often when our children
bring us the things they have made, we pronounce judgment on them—"That's good" or whatever. What if we
were to say first, "Did you enjoy making it? Was it fun to
do?" Then, we could follow with whatever we think of
it. By asking about enjoyment first, we are teaching our
children the important lesson that enjoyment does not
depend totally on another's approval and that the creative
movement outward is a way to earn self-satisfaction.

Another poor attitude we often convey to our children
is putting too much negative emphasis on work: "I have
to work now; leave me alone," as though work cannot
be enjoyable. If we like what we are doing, why not say
instead, "I'd like to work now," and tell the children
why we enjoy it. Most young children will want to help
you. If we habitually tell them to go away and not to
bother us while we are working, we are putting them in
the role of intruders. Working together is a way of learning closeness, responsibility, and how to do things. By
taking the time and effort to teach your children, by allowing them to help, by welcoming their company, you
are showing them your approval and affection, and are
thus pleasing them immensely. If you are doing something which requires concentration and quiet and there
is no appropriate way that they can help, why not tell
them that they may stay with you and do something of
their own that is equally quiet. Being children, their
concentration will not last long and they will wander
off to other things. You can tell them that you are not
finished, you still need quiet, but will do something with
them later.

We can also teach our children how to handle the unpleasant things that we must do. The mother who admit-
tedly despises laundry shouldn't pretend she enjoys it,
but she can take the opportunity to show her children

how to accomplish the unpleasant. "I can't say I like it, but not doing it is worse. We'd all smell pretty awful if we never washed our clothes." By pointing out the consequences of not doing them, you are showing that there is a reason for unpleasant tasks. At the same time, you can show them that the unpleasantness of the tasks can be softened by humor. Involving children in these tasks will further decrease their unpleasantness, because doing a task together puts enjoyment into it. As they grow, children should be given their own tasks appropriate to their age and ability. You will teach them that their help is needed and give them the opportunity to make a tangible contribution to the family as a whole. This will help them have a sense of responsibility and commitment, and promote in them the feeling that "I can do it." All of these are needed to make the most of life.

Society's values have impinged upon our children in such a way that too much emphasis on performance was placed upon sons, while daughters were not taught the value of achievement. With the assertion of women today, the climate is changing for our daughters, and that's good. However, we must not continue to prevent our boys from learning to express their feelings. If you mistakenly believe that a man has it made in our society, consider this: hurt, sorrowful, in tormenting pain, is he allowed to cry? Tears are acceptable, even expected, for a woman. Does a man grieve less? Why can't he cry? Why does he find it so impossible to turn to another and freely say "I need you?" If he does this, he is sometimes viewed as "unmanly," so expression of feeling is discouraged. With this view we develop the bodies and the minds of our sons, but we fail to give them human hearts. Denying them this, we are left with men of action without essentials, hollow shells that dare not show what lies inside. Our smiles, our warmth, our laughter teach our children gladness. We also need to teach our sons and daughters how to handle sadness. If something is troubling us, they can see it. "What's the matter, Daddy?" Too often we say, "Oh, nothing" or "You're too young to understand." Why not tell them, instead, that there are times when we all are hurt or disappointed or sad, and explain it as best we can. If they should hurt us by something they do, why not let them know? If we don't, they will never know how to handle the inevitable hurts that they will have.

Some parents feel that they must never disagree in front of the children; frequently, one parent always gives in to avoid conflict. It is not humanly possible to have an intense relationship between two people without some disagreement. If we always avoid it, how will the children learn that disagreement does not destroy relationships; how will they learn to have a conflict and then to compromise and settle it? Here again balance and appropriateness for the age of the child need to be considered. If we show our children that nothing disastrous happens because we don't agree, if they see that we can compromise and try to negotiate a settlement, we supply them with yet another invaluable lesson in living.

The question of conflict shows again the destructiveness of exaggeration. In the situation where fierce fighting is common, children are trapped. There is nothing they can do but listen and be filled with fear. When this occurs, children are being psychologically abused by two people who know nothing of the human mind and heart. Seeing only that relationships are disastrous, they can learn only rigidity as a way of mastering and will shy away from any kind of feeling relationship. In a situation like this, rather than having two models giving poor impressions, children would be better off with only one. Their chance of learning what they need to know in the primary classroom is small with one poor parent, but it's better than the opportunity they have with two poor parents.

This leads me to the painful subject of divorce. A house filled with strife is not a home. It inflicts intense damage on everybody in it. Remember, our children will not be able to change their pasts any more than we could change ours. If conflict and strife characterize your home, for the children's sake—and each other's—try professional guidance. If that doesn't resolve the problems, give each other and your children a gift. I am deeply committed to marriage as a value, but sometimes people cannot continue to live together. If divorce is necessary, do it without escalating the war to the point of littering the battlefield with broken children. If couples who seek divorce would view their divorce as a mutual gift—a gift of the remaining years of their lives—which each gives the other, then the effect of the divorce on their children would be far less disastrous.

The primary classroom must prepare our children for the secondary one. Children learn not only from us but from the contacts they have outside the home. In their early years, our reaction to what they bring in from the outside world teaches them how to deal with it. For children to make the separation from the primary classroom at an appropriate age, they need to have had enough exposure to the secondary classroom to be able to live in it. Contact with the outside teaches them openness and gives them the opportunity to test their own feelings and ideas within a broader framework. At first, your approval and acceptance of what they learn is the key to whether they take it in or reject it. Unprogrammed time is needed for making and establishing their own relationships and for testing out their own acceptable strivings. Children need freedom of movement appropriate to their age as well as freedom to have their friends around them. Through their peer relationships, children learn about others—how they feel and do things, and how other families react. If we tell our children that we understand, point out that differences in lifestyles are real and acceptable, we are teaching them tolerance and openness.

There is much concern among parents about the bad influence some of their children's friends may have. In the beginning, parental approval of what children bring in from the outside world is the basis for children's selection. We should teach them that not all outside behavior is acceptable to us. Thus, when one of their friends walks on the coffee table, stop him. When he responds with "My mommy lets me," point out the obvious—you are not his mother, nor is he in his own home. By stepping in, you are maintaining the consistency of your own standards, showing your children how to do something about an unpleasant situation, and giving them the guidelines for their friends whom they bring home.

Children's peer relationships bring them into immediate contact with whole family units. They will see and hear about the concerns of others and wonder about the differences. If they come home with a tale of a neighbor's fight, why not use the opportunity to tell them that adults get angry too. Nobody can be calm all the time. Close questioning of children about the details of what they witness in other people's houses, however, could be damaging to their sense of privacy and would only teach your children that gossiping is acceptable.

In preparing them for separation, we must allow our children to try to settle their own problems in their peer relationships. This applies to siblings as well. Too often, for the sake of peace, we step in. If we do this consistently, how will our children learn to solve conflicts for themselves? At times, to prevent a smaller child from being hurt, we must intervene. When we do, we should suggest some alternative ways to settle the dispute and leave it for our children to choose which one they will use.

To raise activators we need to keep the creative movement developing. The smallest children can learn to choose. Offer them two things they like to eat and give them the choice of one or the other. They may want both, but limiting them to one will teach them that they cannot have everything they want and you will be laying the groundwork for future decision making.

As children grow, let the type of decision grow with them. We can, as they get older, help them list the pros and cons of doing something. Teach them to assess the importance of each. A reasonable time limit for deciding is a help, if children have difficulty. Let them miss an occasional opportunity, if they cannot decide. As parents we have to permit children to take the consequences of the decisions they make.

Besides developing their ability to activate, this kind of appropriate freedom of choice teaches children that all decisions need not be made unaided. They can go to others to discover different alternatives. Moreover, this freedom is a powerful parental vehicle for building the sense of trust which is a cornerstone for all close, lasting relationships. The infant and small child, totally dependent as they are, trust parents to provide for their needs. Not only should we, as parents, not betray that trust, but we should trust them in return. If we do not show them this by letting them make appropriate decisions, how can they learn what it is to be trusted?

Despite the current proliferation of books, the loosening of former taboos, the addition of the subject in schools, many parents are still unable to educate their children about sex. Young children who learn from siblings, playmates, and even animals that there are sexual differences need to have their questions answered simply, without parental volunteering of too much information too soon. In an atmosphere which permits questioning, parents will recognize the appropriate answer by the question that is asked. As children need more information, they will ask for more. Without the freedom to question, the child will see sex as forbidden territory, interpreting sex as "wrong" and learning only to avoid the subject.

Parents seem most afraid of the question "Do you do that with Mommy (or Daddy)?" There is a tendency to rely strictly on biological information, thereby neglecting to teach our children the value of sex in the human relationship. Biology will not help parents in this. Nor will many of the available books, which ignore the emotional aspects of sex.

Sex between two people in a close relationship is a personal, private matter. I call this kind of privacy "sexual modesty." As an expression of the unity of their relationship, sex belongs to the two involved, and to them alone. Between two people who are involved in the kind of relationship that is a mutual exchange of warmth, interest, and affection, sex is both an expression of all of these, in the most intimate way, and a nourishment of the relationship as a whole. Revealing too much of one's sexual life will destroy that sense of unity in the relationship.

How then shall we answer our children's questions? At this point, they obviously know some of the biological answers or else they would not be concerned. Detailed descriptions of what their parents do together are unnecessary and inappropriate. The question indicates that the asker is ready to begin to learn the emotional meaning of sexual union.

"Do you do that with Mommy (or Daddy)?"

"Yes, I do and it's beautiful. We try to be as tender and kind to each other as we can be. My pleasing her (or him) pleases me—that's the greatest pleasure—pleasing the one I love."

Eventually, we can tell our children that this kind of satisfaction that we receive from one another not only expresses our relationship but also nourishes it so that the joy we take in pleasing each other affects *them*, too. Given the essentials of life, if our children learn that the greatest pleasure is pleasing the other, they will know how to enjoy sex.

As children grow into adolescence, having been educated in the value of sexuality, it is wise to deal with one of the greatest doubts that youngsters have—and for that matter, that many parents have about their children—homosexuality. Acutely aware of their bodily changes, self-conscious and fearful, children will hesitate to voice their worry. Parents need to initiate the discussion. By not bringing it up, parents give the issue an unreal aura that suggests the despicable and the unmentionable. Having taught them the positive side of sexuality, we need to explain to our adolescents the different forms of sexuality that exist in the secondary classroom. Most of all they need to be reassured about their feelings. Thus, I recommend telling adolescents that there are those who have a strong attraction to the same sex. There is a period in most children's lives when the same sex is more attractive. With growth this usually changes.

Adolescence, the threshold between the primary and the secondary classrooms, is the time for exposure to different varieties of work. If we have already provided our children with opportunities for developing a sense of achievement and the enjoyment of doing things and learning new things, if we have already taught them how to accomplish unpleasant tasks, they are prepared to experiment in the adult working world so that by comparing various jobs, they can reach a decision about their future occupation.

Work is the effort that we put into acquiring the fourth essential (after warmth, interest, and affection), money. Our reward for our work is an adequate supply of money and the satisfaction that comes from having earned it. As parents we should not fear to show our children that we sometimes get fed up with our jobs. Ideally we work at something we like, but no one enjoys his work all the time. Why not talk to our children about our feelings? At times we all get fed up and feel we want to walk away from our commitments. Children can understand this because they have the same feelings —they, too, have days when everything seems to go wrong. By voicing our own feelings, we are showing that those feelings are acceptable and that everyone needs a break from the deadliness of routine.

Within a family, routine can stifle creativity. It makes life too rigid for both parents and children. Nights out, going to new places, doing things with and without the children are necessary to keep routine from becoming exaggerated. Some routine gives stability and security to children, but an inflexible way of doing things, as with anything that is overvalued, deprives rather than helps.

Sometimes it is not possible to take the break we know we need. This becomes an opportunity to teach our children how to wait for what they want. If we keep going despite our need for change, planning for future relaxation at the same time, we are showing our children how to go on despite difficulty.

Adolescents need opportunities for pursuing their

own interests and for experimenting with different kinds of work. This serves a two-fold purpose: the chance to discover where their interests and abilities coincide, and a way to learn how to function in the real world. The ability to work is their passport into the secondary classroom. If they can work, they have the means of acquiring the fourth essential—money.

Work becomes meaningful when it combines effort with the enjoyment gained from personal satisfaction *and* financial reward. Many of us teach our children only about effort and satisfaction and omit educating them in the value of money and its uses. Money is the most common cause of family arguments. Much is neglected in this area, especially for daughters.

When money problems are exaggerated, children learn only the negative. There can never be enough money. If money causes chaos in the family, children will carry into adulthood either the view that they cannot take risks in their work lives for fear of losing what they have, or the view that money is the primary source of pleasure. With either view, money becomes for them, as it was for their parents, an oversensitive issue.

There is no reason why we cannot show our children that money is a necessity and teach them to earn it, explaining that the more we want, the more money we need. Money, because it is tangible, is a tremendous tool for teaching our children that instant gratification in life is not real; they have to learn to wait and put their own effort into gaining the satisfactions that they want. We teach children how to spend money by talking to them about how and why we buy this or that and not another thing, why we shop in one place and not another. Our children will not think less of us when we simply say, "We can't afford to do or buy whatever we would like." It is real to go without something because of lack of money. Why not tell them? They will be learning that some things are possible, others are not. If we talk to our children about our reasons for buying essential things and foregoing luxuries, we are teaching them a system of priority which they will need in order to be sensible users of their own funds.

An allowance or payment for some chores is a useful way of teaching children that even an unpleasant task can have its rewards. Having money of their own, children learn to spend. And they need the freedom to spend a portion of their funds as they wish. I believe that, when-ever possible, they should also have enough money to save for future things. I also believe that we should teach our children how to share their money. Buying their own gifts for friends and relatives is one way. Another is to talk over with them how we support chari-ties, organizations, or other people with financial contri-butions, thus showing them that with money, as with the other essentials, we turn outward, sharing what we have, putting it to greater use.

Given too much money, our children will only learn ex-travagance and waste. Given too little or none at all, they are cheated of learning something they need to know. For many, family financial circumstances are too diffi-cult to permit giving children money. Lack of sufficient funds limits alternatives, but you can explain the cir-cumstances and help children to find opportunities for earning for themselves as soon as they are able. In this case, they must buy necessities for themselves and share their money by contributing to the family as a whole. These children learn in a harder school, but in a friendly and sharing atmosphere, they also learn that money is not the only goal in life.

As parents, we support our children completely in early childhood, but the affluent tend to carry this support too far. Continuation of total support through adolescence will leave children unready for the secondary classroom. Reasonable and appropriate contribution to what they want and need will prepare them better.

Through all the situations I have described, there runs a common theme. We talk to our children and we listen to them in return. We are providing them with the pathway to a good life by giving them understanding and concern, by being open and really hearing them, and by praising them as well as correcting them.

Whatever is learned at home is carried over into the secondary classroom. This connection lasts throughout life. Having learned interchange, the taking in and giving-away of essentials within the family, our children will be prepared to make the necessary separation. Able to make the creative movement outward, they will know how to add on what we have failed to teach them. Able to activate themselves, they will utilize the resources of the secondary classroom in the ongoing process of finding a better way of living.

9/ *A Better Way of Living*

From the steaming corridors of the rain forests to the icy playgrounds of the penguin and the polar bear, from the clear, warm waters of the coral reef to floating ice packs, the very existence of all living things hinges on the beautiful, complex interdependence which is the balance of creation. Disturb that interdependence, destroy the balance, and life is lost. The amount of life that is lost depends on the degree of imbalance.

The interdependence we see in nature is found, too, in all human societies. In all of these, the separation of roles and work is necessary for existence. The more complex the society is, the more specialized the roles become.

While interdependence may be obvious in terms of survival, we may not recognize that it is just as important in terms of the quality of life for each of us individually. If we do recognize the importance of interdependence, we usually see it only in terms of our immediate family. In our goal-oriented society we have highlighted individual achievement and independence. The portrait of the self-made man is held up for all to adulate.

It is evident that those with major weaknesses in

their emotional patterns are turned inward in self-preoc-cupation. Repetitious negative mastering increases this inversion. The overstress in our society on individual performance has been a large factor in causing all of us to turn inward. In the area of individual achievement it-self, the person is isolated by the attitude "It's not my job." Exaggeration of the importance of unaided per-formance prevents people from attempting to activate even in this area of personal performance. Fear of failure is too strong. Also, the fear of a negative response to their attempt to add on a new dimension prevents them from trying to learn something new or developing an unused talent.

The varieties of cultures which are the source of the uniqueness of American society are also the source of the strong tendency for groups to remain aloof. The ten-dency toward aloofness is the result of ignorance and the fear that somehow one group may assault or destroy the heritage of the other. Unfortunately, this group aloof-ness seeps down so that we, individually, tend to hold ourselves separate from anyone who is "different." This, together with the philosophical foundation that over-emphasizes the individual—who *is* unique, important, eminently precious, but who is *also* a member of the human community—results in a pervasive isolationism.

Overemphasis on independence and self-sufficiency permeates our society. Among the poor, the exaggera-tion is softened because their economic and social situa-tion makes independence and self-sufficiency very dif-ficult. But for the bulk of the population, traditional family life has been "phased out" because of emphasis on the individual. Loss of proximity among family mem-bers, because of increasing mobility, has hastened the process. An inversion, a turning inward similar to the in-dividual's, has taken place in the family. The result is a family unit that is tight, controlled, self-sustaining—a pressure cooker without a safety valve. The individual is supposed to learn to fulfill his potential independently within a family unit that relies only on itself.

It used to be that the traditional family provided emotional support, outlets for releasing pressure, and available advice. It had its code—do not shame the family—which was softened by a sense of loyalty and feelings of belonging and acceptance. The broader boundaries of the traditional family, which included all relatives, provided the children with much more chance to learn the differences between appropriate and inappropriate behavior, to learn how one person affects another, and to learn responsibility.

Within this framework, individual achievement was in much better perspective and actually gained more real satisfaction for the doer. Scholastic, artistic, economic, or athletic success reflected on the whole family and won the admiration of all. However, the pressure to be perfect or to be foremost in one's field was not as great because achievement was measured in comparison with the rest of the family not with the rest of society. Moreover, since acceptance did not depend on performance, those with less talent did not feel they had to perform beyond their abilities. Proving the point was the fact that if success was gained at the expense of repudiating the family, family pride in the accomplishment soured. Thus, individuality and *inter*dependence maintained a sensible proportion.

Isolationism and the ensuing erosion of relationships within the family have left us with a family unit which attempts to hold up the remnants of the older code (for example, the traditional religion of the family) without the supporting ties that gave it meaning. At the same time, the "modern" family unit adheres to a new code that demands that it be self-sustaining. Deprived of the means of releasing tensions outside its tight boundaries, it is turned inward in preoccupation with itself.

The very ordinary situation of the only child clearly shows the effect of too tight a family circle. We somehow expect this child to be a little different. I have discussed how children learn by imitating their parents. When all parental attention is focused on the solitary child the intensity of the relationship is overwhelming. All parental expectations become magnified in the child; there is no one else to put one's hopes on. If overindulgence is the family style, the only child gets it all. If performance is the code, there is no one else to relieve some of the pressure; the only child simply must not fail. Thus, intense contact with the secondary classroom from earliest years is mandatory for the only child in order to counterbalance the lack of siblings.

As the traditional family ties fade away, we are losing something essential—we are losing the richness of relationships. The self-sufficient family unit creates inverted, self-centered persons. Husband and wife, never having learned reciprocity themselves, cannot teach it to their children. Within this inverted structure, children learn to view others as sources of instant gratification or as means to be used to achieve individual success. We seem to be creating a society incapable of real enjoyment.

Look at sex, which is supposed to be a source of pleasure for us all. With the breaking down of traditional taboos, unrealistic and destructive as they might have been, it would seem logical that anxiety about sex would be lessened, that more real and natural enjoyment would be heightened. But the opposite is true. Sex is causing as much, if not more, concern than before. It used to be treated as unmentionable, even shameful, but now it has lost its simplicity and meaning. We have destroyed the taboos, but by limiting sex to a biological performance emphasizing self-centered physical pleasures, we have substituted another extreme which is equally destructive. Sex, too, is a victim of exaggerated emphasis on individual achievement. Spontaneity is buried under an avalanche of information on technique, and the pleasure of sex becomes dependent on how it is done. Overconcerned with how we perform, we may end up unable to enjoy sex at all.

If we have lost the meaning of relationship, if we are without the essentials of life, we will not be satisfied with sex regardless of how many books we read or diagrams we follow. We certainly will be unable to teach our children the value of sex, namely, that its true enjoyment stems from *mutual* pleasure, from reciprocal giving and receiving. This kind of feeling is impossible outside a close relationship built on mutual warmth, interest, and trust. Sex is both a deep and pleasurable expression of that relationship and a source of its nourishment.

Just as preoccupation with self is robbing sex of its meaning, the inversions and tightness this preoccupation causes within the family may well be a direct cause of the high divorce rate. The rigidity of the self-sufficient family unit allows no room for release of tension between spouses. Each represses resentments. When one is able to tolerate and adapt to the accumulated stress he or she becomes stronger than the other. One partner outgrows the other. When the distance between the two is widened sufficiently, separation or divorce may follow.

In the past decade there has been growing discussion of the breakdown of the family, but the alternatives being suggested beg the question. Communal living (which may work for a small minority) is one attempt to relieve the pressure. Living together without the commitment of marriage is another. For many, these solutions are self-defeating as they maintain each person in a self-sufficient position without a real sense of belonging that a close, committed, mutual relationship brings.

The feminist movement is contributing to the destruction of the family. It is making a real and much needed contribution to society with its insistence on equality for women. Without equality in an adult relationship, there can be no real reciprocity of feeling. However, by overemphasizing individual female achievement—such as in careers for women—it fails to credit women with their most basic and natural source of power. As I have said previously, the most potent controlling force in all our lives, be we male or female, is our relationship with our mothers. If women ignore or denigrate this aspect of their sexuality, they deny themselves tremendous personal gratification and deny their children the proper foundation for their future relationships. Without the feeling "I can do it," there is incompleteness. But overemphasis on individual achievement for women without awareness of interdependence or of the real importance of motherhood will undermine this first relationship, robbing women of their greatest power and influence, producing, in the long run, a society of robotlike people.

We will all regret in old age our preoccupation with self. To whom shall we turn? The family no longer feels responsible for the elderly. In losing relationships, we have apparently lost the ability to enthusiastically and joyfully celebrate with one another our times of success and gladness. We have also lost support in times of need or sorrow. Turned inward, we rob ourselves of life's pleasures and leave ourselves alone and unsupported in times of pain.

Moving is a fact of life in today's society. Statistics

indicate that fifty percent of the population does not live in the state of their birth. Twenty percent have moved every year over the past twenty years. The contribution that this kind of mobility makes to the breakdown of family and friendship relationships cannot be ignored. The attitude "We move so often, all we have is each other. We're very close" is symptomatic of the isolated family. To reverse this inversion we must work within the framework that divides families and friends by long distance and be creative about keeping contacts open. There is no reason why we cannot activate in this area; the risk is nonexistent, the rewards great.

Our culture is built on the family unit. With technological and industrial complexity came super-movement, and we have lost the extended family as a result. Who takes the place of aunts, uncles, sisters, brothers who live halfway across country? No one, if we have no friends. The pioneers depended on one another for survival. We need our friends for our emotional survival in today's society. Unfortunately, we seem to have lost the art of making friends, sharing good times, helping one another in bad times, and learning from others. It has no overtones of sex or romance, no element of control of one by the other, no obligation made or demanded. Friendship is a mutual sharing and caring, respect and trust. Tensions, disappointments, arguments may happen. They may shatter a weak friendship; they will not destroy a solid one.

We have ignored our interdependence far too long. Overemphasis on independence is depriving us of the resources for softening our individual exaggerations, for adding on what we failed to learn in the primary classroom, and for giving our lives the quality we seek. There is an obvious interdependence between the species of life in nature. Social interdependence is also apparent in the community of mankind. Philosopher, doctor, farmer, street cleaner, all are part of the web that gives society its balance. In the emotional sphere, interdependence can be denied, but the quality of our lives will be diminished. Here, too, a balance is needed between the individual as a single person and as a member of a group, who in relationships alternately supports and is supported.

All activation, the creative outward movement unique in ourselves, seeks a response because we are interdependent in all the spheres of life. If individual achievement is our deficiency, the resources available are tremendous. Schools of all kinds, community programs, recreational facilities, all are there. But do we really achieve alone? With encouragement, support, working together, we achieve more. Without other satisfactions and without a positive response our work can succeed, but money alone will not satisfy us.

No one is without limitations, completely self-satisfying and self-sufficient. This is the path of inversion, and we see its results all about us. The other avenue was there in childhood. A child is not ashamed to say "I need you." Why are we? A child can say, "I just want to be with you." Why can't we? A child is not afraid to say "I like you" or "I love you." Why are we? The child is learning to have a close relationship, but will growth continue?

Friendship is the most accessible resource available to add on what we do not know and improve the quality of our lives. There are others all around us. As children we admired and imitated qualities we liked in others in a natural process of growth. For some people this process came to a halt.

Our homes were the primary classrooms for our emotional education, our parents the primary teachers. The neighborhood, the street, the school, the community in which we lived, all combined to make our secondary classroom. Our friends were our teachers, too.

For the small child, friendship is spontaneous and natural. He learns quickly to share, to fight, to make up, to share again. Go to the beach and bring a four-year-old. Watch him digging in the sand, constructing fabulous fortresses, castles with moats. Look quickly, he won't be alone long. Another will come to join him, perhaps more. It may seem like hours to you in the burning sun, with grit in your bathing suit, but ask *him*.

"I had the best time, Daddy. I made a new friend."

"That's great. What's his name?"

Blank look, small shrug of sunburned shoulders.

"Oh, I don't know."

He doesn't know; he didn't need to know. Maybe next time he'll think to ask but they were too busy. Interest in each other came so quickly that names were unimportant. The feeling was there.

On the street, in the neighborhood, eventually at school, children make friends with each other with a naturalness and spontaneity that can be inhibited by parental attitudes. Having or being a friend is one of the most natural strivings of all children. We don't have to teach them to seek out friends; we have to teach them to stay home. Parents can give a child the impression that there is something wrong with being close to others so that the child is unable to recognize his acceptable striving. Overscheduling and rigidity can destroy the naturalness of childhood friendships. By making friendship a ritual, parents take the relationship out of their children's hands. In such a situation children may learn the art of friendship less well.

In adolescence—that time of testing—the young person is caught between childhood and maturity, and the energy of friendship is at its peak. Strengths and weaknesses mirrored in one's friends provide a testing ground for new ideas. Friends can be unkind and hurt you, but friends can also give support to shaky self-esteem, and can wipe away fears of being alone. The last years before responsibility, the last years of dependence on parents, adolescence also marks the last period that naturalness and spontaneity can be clearly seen. The peer group is far more diversified, far more natural than it will ever be again.

We lose childhood's kind of friend-making as we become adults. With all growth, as the old disappears something new can be gained. In losing childhood's naturalness we can add on awareness and concern for the feelings of others. Developing these, we learn compassion, consideration, and kindness. Too often as adolescence wanes, we grow too close to the goal of independence. Unaided resolution of problems, making it on our own, an "I'd-rather-do-it-myself" attitude are all part of the goal, which overemphasizes individualism. Cultural, racial, and economic factors also work against the extension of friendship into adulthood.

In adulthood, opportunities for making new friends can seem harder to find. We can buy everything we need. We don't need to rely on others for their skills in everyday living; instead, we pay workers for their skill. Common interests and helping each other keep a society strong, but as adults we tend to limit ourselves to situational friendships which overemphasize common interest. We base our search for friends on our work, limit it to our neighborhood or to the PTA. If we find it hard to get close to those who are in the same circumstances, or find them boring, we look no further, but go without friends, unless we have a crisis. Crisis-oriented groups such as Alcoholics Anonymous, Weight Watchers, or the

like, offer opportunities for friendship. Perhaps it is because our problems make us aware once again that we
really do need one another. Why do we wait? We are
missing all the fun.

With the loss of the extended family, the stress on the
family unit, and our tendency to be preoccupied with
ourselves, we are left alone too much. We don't even
know how to get started at making friends. We assume
that people will not be interested in us. Since they, in
turn, have the same feeling, no one does anything. Fear
of exposing our weaknesses, fear of taking the risk, fear
of being hurt makes us all too cautious in opening ourselves to others.

In meeting people, we tend to rationalize our unwill-
ingness to reveal ourselves by the statement "We don't
have anything in common." What we really seem to mean
is: "We don't have everything in common." All that we
really need to have in common is a mutual interest in
each other and a mutual understanding of each other.
Beyond that, differences, instead of being inhibitors, can
be opportunities for opening new avenues of knowledge
and for learning new ways of mastering as we imitate
our friends.

In old age, as approaching death becomes the equalizer,
as fear of loneliness gives us the impetus, a physical
frailty forces on us an awareness of our need for others.
There is often a new, more insistent search for friends.
Out of common need, differences in race, belief, or
economic status seem to lose their importance. The
elderly achieve equality by helping each other. They are
interdependent, and there is reciprocity of feeling and
support, which allows friendship to flourish once again.

Friendship is a singular kind of relationship. In all real
friendships, there is a reciprocity unattached to tangi-

ble things that makes friendship unique among all other close relationships. We did not choose our parents, but we choose our friends. There is a further difference. Between two friends, neither controls the other. Our parents controlled us and we were dependent on them.

Magazine articles and commercial advertisements to the contrary, being true friends with your children before their maturity is impossible. Care, respect, warmth, and interest should be there, but there is a missing ingredient—equality. The relationship is lopsided by its nature. Parents determine what their children should do and see that they do it. Children are dependent upon and controlled by their parents. It is possible, and beautiful when it happens, for an adult child to add on a friendship relationship with a parent. This takes place only by mutual choice and with a kind of putting aside of the former relationship.

Friendship is sexless. When, or if, we make a lover of a friend, the relationship changes. Adding on physical intimacy alters the quality of a friendship, forming a different kind of relationship. The most solid foundation of a marriage is an adding-on of a friend relationship to the love relationship. The equality, mutual trust, and respect, the feeling of being comfortable with the other person, and the reciprocity of the friend relationship are the essentials which nourish the love relationship and give it longevity. Without being friends, lovers will eventually watch their relationship wither and die. When both relationships are combined, there is a real and lasting marriage relationship—something different from friendship.

Our first tentative overtures in making new friends are an activation. We are turning outward, seeking a response. As the other gives away interest in us, we take it in and respond again. We deepen the friendship by continuing the interchange on new levels. If we really take in our friend and make him or her a part of us, the relationship weaves itself through the very fabric of our emotional pattern, strengthening our weaknesses as we add a new dimension to our lives. The beauty of friendship lies in this and in the fact that we are doing the same for our friends by simply being ourselves.

Afraid to say "I need you," "I like you," "I miss you" when distance divides us, we want close relationships and are disappointed and hurt when others do not respond. How can they know if we do not tell them? In today's society we need our friend relationships more than ever before. Who else can be our surrogate family? There is no other resource that is as accessible to everyone to give life the meaning we seek. We knew so well in childhood the importance of our friends. Why have we failed to carry this kind of relationship into adulthood?

Courtship and marriage seem to break the bonds of friendship—and we don't return to pick them up again. Nor do we, having lost old friends, turn to make others with the same kind of openness we had in youth.

In courtship and marriage we become preoccupied with a single person. In the beginning we tend to feel that the one we love is all that is, or ever will be, necessary. Romance in its unreal sense doesn't last, but we continue the preoccupation with the other person as we adjust to marriage. Adjustments are necessary as we plan out and improve upon the primary classroom for our children. Our aim should be to establish a friendly atmosphere, a place where our own feelings and frailties as well as our children's can be exposed and discussed with room for warmth and humor. Without diminishing the importance or necessity of these adjustments, we should and can keep our friendships nourished. Unfortunately, we tend to fall into a routine of family life and work that avoids outside relationships—an avoidance that our children will be likely to imitate. In our preoccupation with one person, with our families, or with our work, we expect to find all our emotional needs satisfied—an unrealistic expectation. We make the boundaries of our lives too small and tight by expecting ourselves and our families to be self-sufficient.

Courtship is a necessary period. It is a time for seeking out the type of person we would like to live with in the most intense of all relationships. Preoccupation with each other is natural in this time of sunshine and soft rain, special dreams and feelings that are new to us. Saplings promise stately trees. Can these sprouts grow strong season after season, able to weather winds that break the weaker branches, droughts that threaten shallow roots? Can we nourish this promise of a lifelong relationship so that its roots grow deep, its branches reaching further toward the sky as the passing years bring new growth?

Courtship is a time for exploring another person, a time of testing to discover when we can build a marriage. This is a question which cannot be answered lightly. Here, openness about our feelings and values, likes and dislikes, strengths and weaknesses, hopes and fears is essential. We have to use this time for careful thought, negotiation, assessment of ourselves and the other before we decide to marry.

Marriage, that intense, intimate combination of the love relationship and the friend relationship, can be a most valuable resource for adding on what we do not know and giving life its meaning. Above all, it is an adult relationship between two persons, both of whom are activators who contribute their creativity to nourishing the relationship in a constant mutual interchange of all four essentials of life.

With all change in life, we lose something in order to gain something else. By marrying, we lose our freedom. We gain the opportunity to make our lives together in an upward spiral of giving and receiving. Like all close relationships, marriage should strive to be unselfish. Pleasing the other is a source of our pleasure. If our marriage is merely an extension of our childhood way of life, it will turn inward. If we have to see ourselves as independent, if we cannot say "I love you" and "I need you," our marriage will have no meaning and no life. If we fail to nourish the relationship, the marriage cannot survive.

The intensity of the marriage relationship affects all areas of the lives of the two individuals. Its very closeness demands a turning outward. The creative movement of each individual seeks self-enrichment within the relationship, the enrichment of the other individual, and the growth of the relationship itself. No two people can live together without disagreement. Turned outward to the world around them, they find release for inevitable tensions. What each gives and receives, what together they give and receive from the outside world nourishes the relationship, giving it the flexibility to adapt to the inevitable changes time brings.

I have spoken of parenthood as the adding on of a new dimension. While our children cannot be our friends in an adult relationship, our closeness with our children is yet another resource. I have spoken at length about what we give them, but any close relationship is an interchange. What do our children give to us? Are we open to receive what they offer so uninhibitedly? In great fullness they give us the feeling that we are needed. They teach us, or reawaken in us, the excitement of learning, a joy in the world around us, which they see with shiny newness. They give us laughter and lessons in how to play, things we tend to lose with tedium. They chase away boredom, that lethal stifler of life. By imitating them, we can add on, or regain, a spontaneity and exuberance in living. If we find it hard to express our feelings, we can learn from them to say "I love you." We give them much, teach them much, endure much for them—that is as it should be. They will return much during childhood if we are receptive. How much greater can the return be when they have separated from us! We lose our children when they make their own emotional separation, but we gain adults. With adulthood, they must accept us as we are. Can we not accept them? No longer children, we can meet them on common ground as equals. The relationship changes, but it need not lose its closeness.

We have come full circle back to friendship as the most accessible resource of all. It forms the cornerstone of our other close relationships and nourishes them as well. We learn it first on the childhool level, and in learning it we find equality and openness. As we grow with each new friend, we have the chance of adding on to ourselves. Throughout life, there are other people. The give and take with them is at once life's greatest resource and its source of meaning. Turned inward we miss too much. Pain and sorrow, frustration, and disappointment, all are real and unavoidable. Can we not do something about them and balance life with pleasure, joy, and achievement? We can put aside the myth of independence and self-sufficiency and recognize the true proportions of life. Solitary achievement is not enough; sharing life is the better way.

We can be activators; we can use our creativity in all

the spheres of life. We can turn outward to give and receive warmth, interest, affection, and money in the ongoing process of truly human living. Facing reality—
involved in its good and its bad—accepting ourselves and
our interdependence, building up, not tearing down—
there really *is* a better way of living.